Bill Bramah's

ONTARIO

BOOK IV

Bill Bramah's

ONTARIO

BOOK IV

by

Bill Bramah

CANNONBOOKS
MISSISSAUGA

Copyright ©1994 by Bill Bramah

Published by: CANNONBOOKS
                       3710 Nashua Drive
                       Mississauga, Ontario L4V 1M5

Canadian Cataloguing in Publication Data
   Bramah, Bill, 1915 -
      Bill Bramah's Ontario, Book IV

   ISBN 0-9695251-3-3

   1.   Ontario - Biography - Anecdotes.   2. Ontario - History,
   Local - Anecdotes. I. Title.

   FC3061.8.B73 1994   971.3'002   C94-932667-4
   F1057.6.B73   1994

Design and Production by: Michael Waldin
Illustrations by: John Jacques

First Printing: April, 1995

Front Cover:The plasticine sculpture was done by Bryan Stewart for a cover story in the Toronto Star's "Starweek" Magazine. Photo of the sculpture by Mel Loynd from an original photo by Linda Chernecki.

Acknowledgments

First and foremost is my wife Jenny, the tireless production assistant who's been my right hand since the beginning. Then there's cameraman Rick Dade. When Rick couldn't make it, Kevin Smith would be there, or upon occasion John Whyle, Mark Foerster, Doug Gamey or Sandy Piminoff. Since I write in restaurants, truck stops, hotels, motels, or anywhere I hang my hat, all in longhand, the stories have been meticulously deciphered and typed by Angela Barker, the gal with the bear-trap mind on Global's promotional staff. The head honcho of the department, Dave Hamilton, has been plugging my efforts since we both went with the network two decades ago. In the publicity field, Dave can pull rabbits out of hats. Talented designer Michael Waldin put the book together from an tangled mess of stories, photos and illustrations I handed him. Finally a tip of the hat to artist John Jacques and to Linda Chernecki for her top-flight photos. Bless 'em all.

Contents

Cottage Country and the North

Reaching for the Moon 15
Donkeys Unlimited 17
Stella's Idea 18
School of Falconry 20
The Candlemakers 21
Bigwin Inn 24
Bill's Impossible Dream 26
Resident's Choice 27
B.B. and His Fish 29
Kindergolf 31
Born in a Barn 33
The Friendly Giant 34
Big Bus Company 35
Blinking Shoes 37
Carousel Restorer 39
Lucy's Holiday 40
The Honey King 42
Santa Carver 44
Benny's Mine 45
Marble Mine 48
The Hole 49
Labour of Love 51
Colette's Hacienda 54
Celebrity Socks 56
The Phillumenist 57
Old Town Gets a Facelift 59
Porcupine Quilling 61

Western Ontario

Mennonite Market 65

Scottish Heritage 67

Little Library .69

Local Hero 71

Big Time in Miniature 73

Frank's Garden 75

Dave and Seaweed 77

The Bag Lady .79

The Backus Mill 81

Family of Newsies 83

Ernie's Peanuts 84

Wooden Wonders 85

The Gentle Barbarian 87

Summer Gardens 88

Easter Egg Chickens 90

Computer Composer 92

Mainly Because of the Heat 93

The Great Law .95

Creative Carvers 97

Flyball Winners 98

Lily Beck 100

Lifestyles of the Rich and Feathered 102

Clock Watchers 104

Surprise Sarnia 105

Canada's Oldest Private Eye 107

Ontario's Best Kept Secret 109

Central and Eastern Ontario

Tyrone Mill 115
The Smallest Jail 117
A Magic Piano 118
The Old Master .120
The Perfect Butter Tart 122
Ponderosa 124
Detector's Dream 125
Junk Art 127
Field of Dreams .129
Barn Raising 131
Cookstown Greens 132
Willie the Bull .134
The Old Sport Co. 136
A Curious Business Venture 137
Have Camels, Will Travel 139
The Little Rebel 141
Barrie Clipper .144
Flower Sculpture 145
Jack's Train 147
Decoy Champs 149
Vintage Phonographs 150
The Right Stuff .153
Stamp of Approval 154
House of Dolls .156
The Simple Life .158
When The Heat's On 160
Sugarbush Bunnies 162
Ontario's Breadbasket 164
The Queen Bead .166
Ken's Collection 167
The Artisans 170
Spinning Wheels .171
Firefighter's Museum 173

Introduction

❦

Back in the heady days of razzle-dazzle journalism, I was a brash young newshawk addicted to what's known in the business as "hard copy" or in some quarters "meaningful news."

This includes wars, rumors of wars, politicians spouting irrelevant rhetoric, murders, fires, accidents and other assorted versions of misery and mayhem.

Later, when I went with Global, my interests shifted slightly. I began to look for more off-beat items, but always within the mosaic of the city, my natural habitat. I liked the kaleidoscope of its many faces and myriad moods. I looked for the exotic, the extraordinary, amid the hurly-burly and frenetic face of it all.

Then, almost by chance, I discovered country roads. They're not like harsh, flat, multi-lane highways. Country roads keep the rise and fall of the land. They twist and turn and you get the feeling that the first human path was beaten by feet not quite sure of their direction.

The wandering roads slowed me down. I mellowed. I took a new look at the simplicity and joy of country life and the easier ways of small town Ontario. I found that the ordinary can become the extraordinary, and that smiles 'n chuckles are survival tools desperately needed in our lives. I also learned to sense the vibrant vitality of the North, to bask in the beauty of the Bay of Quinte area, to walk and talk with Mennonite families, and swap stories with the fisherfolk of Lake Erie's north shore.

With my wife Jenny as production assistant, and more recently our buddy, veteran cameraman Rick Dade, I've travelled hundreds of thousands of miles over the years to see the places and meet the people I've written about in this book, and the three others that have gone before it.

Some of the people you'll meet are inspiring. Some are just plain fun. But all of them and their hometowns provide a different side of news — a lighter, more human side. It's part of the legacy of country life that leads you to another Ontario.

Bon voyage.

Cottage Country and the North

Reaching for the Moon

❦

I'm not a mechanical man. Mechanically I'm a dud. My philosophy in mechanical matters has always been "let George do it." But when I met Dr. Ted Sparrow and he began a rapid-fire show-and-tell outline of his super-dooper ham radio set-up, I decided to learn something.

Dr. Sparrow is an expert in this field. He's famous among amateur radio buffs. He writes books and articles. He knows his stuff. So I concentrated. I took notes. I looked wise. But as he expounded technical data, my mind became clogged, boggled and bewildered.

It was understandable. Dr. Sparrow has a bear trap brain and knows a lot about a lot of things. He's not an electrical or mechanical engineer. He's a dentist! He's about 60 and left an established practice in the city and opened another practice near the hamlet of Allenwood in the Elmuale area.

He and his wife Sandie have converted the old Allenwood schoolhouse into a luxurious dwelling. As soon as you drive up to it you realize there's more than just dentistry going on in there. Four antennae reach up toward the sky. Two of them, I learned, are what are called "moon bouncers." That means they can bounce radio signals off the moon to reach ham operators from Europe to Hawaii. And one of the bouncers is the largest in the country.

Dr. Ted and Sandie, who is also a licenced operator, took me up to the control room on the second floor of the schoolhouse. It was packed with sophisticated electronic equipment. They pointed out the uses of a variety of complex gadgets and I responded with such profound statements as "Well, isn't that interesting." Or I'd raise

Ted and Sandie Sparrow baffled Bill with their far-ranging knowledge of electronics, astronomy and photography, among other things.

my eyebrows and say "Really?" to show my apparent comprehension of the complicated array of dials and gauges.

But that was only the beginning. We went into another room where there was a bank of computers. This was their "electronic bulletin board" where they send messages to "computer nuts" as they call them.

The tour continued to the rec room, where there was a maze of photographic gear. Dr. Ted teaches photography and the couple have made up a spectacular slide show about Huronia which they take to schools and special events. Then it was over to look at some of their show dogs, and later their astronomy telescopes.

While all this was going on, Dr. Ted said, "I forgot to tell you we'll soon be able to send out more powerful radio signals. We're getting a dish next week."

One reason the dynamic duo left the city was because of the high density of sound. Now that they're out in the country it will be easier to reach for the moon. And when the new dish arrives, the Sparrows will be flying high.

Getting There

The Sparrows live a few miles west of Elmvale, which is about 20 miles north of Barrie on Highway 27. The address is RR# 2 Elmvale L0L 1P0.

Donkeys Unlimited

❦

I learned a lot about donkeys recently. The humble donkey (Equus Asinus) was domesticated long before the horse, and evolved from wild bands roaming in Africa. Donkeys, burros, asses, are all the same animal. A mule is different. It results from the mating of a horse (a stallion) and a donkey, or a male donkey and a mare.

I learned all this from John Hemsted and Henry Regelink, partners in a venture called "Donkeys Unlimited" in Oro Township south of Orillia. They import donkeys from Texas and sell them to sheep farmers here.

Donkeys are in great demand these days to protect sheep from predators such as wolves or coyotes. Ordinarily, donkeys are gentle, docile creatures, but they bare their teeth and lash out with their hooves if a wolf, coyote or wild dog comes sneaking around.

The first time I saw donkeys protecting sheep was down around the Bay of Quinte a few years ago where a shepherd has three donkeys guarding his big flock. At that time it was something of a rarity in Ontario. But guard donkeys are becoming increasingly common on sheep farms, and "Donkeys Unlimited" has been doing a brisk business.

John went down to Texas where they've been using donkeys to watch sheep for over 150 years. "They were surprised that the idea was new to us," said John. "They'd never think of raising a sheep without having a donkey around."

As a first move, the partners had 20 females brought up to Big Curve Acres farm in Oro where Henry keeps horses. The females or Jennys (Jennets is the correct name) are far more effective for protection purposes than the males, know as Jacks. John and Henry sold the first lot in no time, and when I was there another group of 30 had just arrived. Off by himself was Texas Tyrone, the only Jack among them. A big, spotted donkey, he will sire additional stock.

There are three general sizes of the friendly animals. The so-called mammoth, the standard which is usually the kind used for protection, and the miniature that's ideal for children to ride.

The sheep seem to love the donkeys and the big bad wolf had better beware. The gentle Jennys can suddenly become hell on hooves if predators try to attack their wooly little buddies.

Getting There

Big Curve Acres is on Highway 11, south of Orillia. But phone first. The number is 705-487-2000. You'll get a kick out of the donkeys.

Stella's Idea

W hen Stella Quesnelle's six children grew up and left home, she was stuck with a chore she didn't like. She was the only one left to rake the one acre yard around the family's home near the Georgian Bay village of Penetanguishene.

It was a tedious task, and she'd mutter to herself as she raked away and her hands started to blister.

One day, while clearing pine cones and debris from the big lawn, she visualized a rake on wheels, like those on a training bicycle. She mentioned the idea to her husband, Al, who operates a welding business in a shop behind the house. Al just laughed. So did her kids when they heard about it.

That didn't phase Stella one bit. She kept after Al and finally persuaded him to use his expertise to help her figure out some alternative to the ordinary rake.

They worked on the idea, and eventually same up with a prototype. Al mounted wheels on a labor-saving rake and added a comb so that the teeth would catch debris, then raise up when pushed ahead. You didn't have to lift the rake at all. Along with that, it had a sponge-covered handle, and a loop on the end so you could hang it up.

They made a few rakes and gave them to friends to use. The response was so positive they made some more and distributed them to area hardware stores at a suggested retail price of $39.00.

Then they got bigger ideas. They began the lengthy process of applying for a patent. Stella got some direction from the Women's Inventions Association and did a patent search in Europe and the United States.

Meanwhile, they've turned out about a thousand rakes for nearby markets, and have big plans for the future of their product which they call the Lawn Star Rake. Al spends most of his spare time assembling the rakes, and he's not laughing at Stella's idea anymore. Neither are the kids.

Getting There

Stella and Al live on Con. 13, Tiny Township near Penetanguishene. Give them a call at 705-549-3625 to get directions from wherever you happen to be. It's not too far from our farm.

School of Falconry

A large falcon was perched on my wrist, his huge talons grasping the heavy falconer's glove I was wearing. He glared at me over his hooked beak. He had a wild look in his eyes. But there was nothing to fear. Two master falconers were at my side, giving me instructions as I held on to a restraining rope for dear life. Anyway, the falcon was trained and used to novices like me.

All this took place at a school of falconry at Golden Creek Bird Farm near Seven Bridge a few miles north of Orillia. The school was started by Fred Hoesterey and Matt Leiberknecht, two European-trained falconers who have been around birds since childhood. They have about 65 birds of prey, including hawks and eagles, along with falcons. Most of the birds were born and raised right at the farm.

The partners in the enterprise not only teach falconry for sport and hunting, but provide bird control services for such places as airports, cities, landfill sites, crop protection and marinas. They also give free flight demonstrations and educational services for schools.

As we walked around the farm we saw majestic golden eagles, breeding pairs of bald eagles isolated in large cages and red-headed hawks. But it's the long line of tethered falcons that catch the eye. There are species like the peregrine, prairies, lanners and an imported saker, the largest of the European species.

There's a nursery where the falcons are bred by both artificial insemination in incubators and the first clutch of eggs from mating birds. There were fluffy baby falcons just 10 days old that were still being fed by hand. Falcons double their weight every week, and nearby was a seven-week-old bird that was about 14 inches tall.

We went outside and Matt showed me a falcon in action. He removed the restraining cord from his wrist and the big prairie falcon he had been holding soared up into the air. In a few moments Matt called out and the falcon zoomed down and landed back on his wrist.

I thought about trying to hold the falcon on my wrist again. Then Matt casually mentioned that the birds can travel at 200 kilometers an hour! I decided to put off the idea until sometime in the future. That's just not my speed.

Getting There

Take Highway 11 north. A few miles past Orillia take the Con 12 exit. Go west and about a mile along the road you'll see a sign on the left directing you to the school. Phone 705-689-9121. The birds are big and beautiful. And fast-feathered bullets. It's open from May to Sept.

The Candlemakers

When Bob Francis was a student at Queen's University, he became interested in making candles. As he says, it was a "trendy thing" at the time.

After graduation, he became an accountant. But the desire to make candles began to smoulder again. With a couple of buddies and a small investment, the trio opened a candle making business at a former farm called Rich Hill near Orangeville.

As time went on, he and his wife, Barbara, bought out the partners and moved the business to the Muskoka town of Bracebridge.

They kept the Rich Hill name and now operate a candle-making business that attracts visitors from various parts of the province.

It's a fascinating set-up. There's a visitors gallery overlooking the production room where you can see candles being make in the traditional way. There's absolutely no automation. Everything is done with old hand-operated machines.

Wax is melted in five big kettles. Then, with the precision of a master chef, Bob conjures up the day's special in colours and fragrances, dropping them carefully into the brew. Thirty different colours are available in fragrances like cranberry, raspberry and green apple.

To make votive candles, wax is scooped up and poured into a trough. It flows like a babbling brook into small containers embedded in the trough. Votive candles have roots deep in medieval times and you may have seen them in some churches.

To create pillar candles, the wax is poured into special moulds. Some of the candles are about two feet high and will burn for four hundred hours.

But I found the process of making taper candles, the ones more familiar to us, the most dramatic of all. Wicks are strung between metal rings. After that, they're hung on a taper-dripping carousel. There are about twenty units that look like bird cages and they go round and round, up and down, being dipped in wax. After thirty dips for colour and two for fragrance, they become the finished products.

Rich Hill can turn out five thousand candles a day. If they went into automation they could do far better than that. But Bob and Barb prefer to keep it simple and retain the romance of the old ways.

They're right, too. With the hassles of big business, they might find themselves burning the candle at both ends. Besides, visitors love the place the way it is, and when I last looked over at the retail section, sales were still burning.

Getting There

Take Highway 11 north to Bracebridge. The first cut-off is Vancoughnet. Turn off and almost immediately turn left. You're on Robert Dottar Drive. Keep going til you see Leon's Furniture on the left. Rich Hill is right across the road.

Bigwin Inn

❦

I always regarded my big brother as quite a sophisticated man-about- town. In the early '30s, he was a successful young bachelor dentist who drove a sporty convertible and on weekends would sometimes take off for spots like Harlem's famed Cotton Club or Muskoka's Bigwin Inn. I was only about 15 and would be very impressed as he relayed stories about such glamorous places.

I was never able to get to the Cotton Club, but recently I visited Bigwin Inn with Doug McIntaggart, who was writing a book about the resort that once was the jewel among Muskoka's many outstanding summer hotels.

Doug and I took a boat from Dorset to Bigwin Island to see the place, but the Inn was a far cry from what I'd heard from my big brother. It's grandeur was gone. It's now a deserted ramshackle wreck. The floors have buckled. For some reason, a grand piano still stands in the rotunda. Mice have nested in it. It's all ghostly. It's eerie.

But Doug was telling me that when it opened in 1920, Bigwin dwarfed all of the other resorts in Muskoka. It was the ultimate in elegance and splendour. Built by C. O. Shaw, an eccentric entrepreneur, it was designed as a playground for the rich, the powerful and the famous.

It could accommodate 500 guests and there were 500 employees to serve them. People came by boat, by train, by plane to the fabulous showplace set in the wilderness. The guests included Queen Juliana, the Rockefellers, Clark Gable and Carole Lombard. Big name bands played in the magnificent pavilion. Continental chefs prepared gourmet dishes. The works!

Doug thinks the decline and fall of Bigwin was caused by changing management and changing times. But many of the people of Muskoka had never seen such gracious, luxurious living, and those that were around during the heyday of the resort still tell endless stories about it.

However, there's a glimmer of hope that it could be restored. Doug says a study is being done to see if it would be feasible to revive the old place and a group of financiers are awaiting the outcome.

Bigwin was at its best during the '20s and '30s. But right now you get the feeling that maybe the Great Gatsby, the cast and the film crew wrapped it up, packed their bags and moved away leaving nothing but a deserted movie set.

Doug's book is on the market. Called ''Bigwin Inn,'' it's published by Boston Mills Press. It's an excellent book, lavishly illustrated, and gives the complete Bigwin story. What remains of the showplace can be seen if you rent a boat at Dorset. But get a knowledgeable guide.

Bill's Impossible Dream

Have you ever had the urge to explore the wilderness in your own bush plane? A plane you built yourself?

I've never had what you'd call an urgent urge to fulfill such a dream. I have a hard enough time battling my old buddy Highway 401. But more intrepid types have done it with kits from Zenaire, a company that supplies plans and parts for first-time builders of light planes.

The idea was a brainchild of a brilliant aeronautical engineer named Chris Heintz. A graduate of the famed E.T.H. Institute in Switzerland, he helped build the Concord, and when he came to Canada, was an aircraft consultant. But in his spare time, while tinkering around in his garage, he began to delve into the feasibility of building kits for planes. That was about 18 years ago. Today, Chris has a plant on the outskirts of Midland where he and his staff of 17 skilled craftsmen turn out about 100 kits a year and an average of 30 custom-made planes.

Chris was the originator of the kits. Before that, you could get plans to build a plane, but you had to go all over hell's half acre to get the parts. But now, Zenaire sends you both plans and parts in a carton, and thousands have been shipped to various parts of the world.

I watched the craftsmen making parts from raw materials. The metal was sheared to size on a computerized machine. The ribs were made by hand, the gas tank welded, skin was rolled over the wings and fuselage, a motor was installed and the plane painted. It takes about 350 hours if you do it yourself.

Zenaire has two models. One is called the Stol and the other the Zodiac. Chris took me for a spin in a Stol. We were off the ground in four seconds. The planes need only 100 feet or so for takeoff. I was surprised and impressed. We hovered over the pines of the southern Georgian Bay area. Suddenly I visualized myself flying my own Stol into Northern Ontario bush country. I was a rugged woodsman just as intrepid as they come. Just as adventurous and dedicated as those who have built their own planes. I, too, had spent hours building my Stol.

Then I was jerked back to reality. I remembered my trouble with Highway 401. I remembered my difficulties trying to build a model airplane when I was a boy, and how my big brother had to help me finish it. I was thinking maybe discretion should be the greater part of valour.

Nevertheless, the dream returns from time to time. And who knows? Perhaps some day fate will get me airborne after I build my Stol. If I run into trouble, Chris can help me, the way my big brother did.

Getting There

One way to get to Midland is to take Highway 11 north to Orillia. Then go west on Highway 12. Its about 30 miles to Midland. Keep going to the junction of Highways 12 and 93. You'll see sign directing you to the airport. The Zenaire plant is beside it.

Resident's Choice

Every year when the sap starts running, I'm off to see what's new in the maple syrup industry. There's usually nothing new really. Oh, I've seen a pretty snazzy sugar bush near Bancroft operated by a computer. But other than the now-familiar plastic tubing that carries the sap to the sugar sacks, not very much has changed in the harvesting process in half a century.

Then I met Peter Harris. He and his dog live on a farm near the Southern Georgian Bay village of Victoria Harbour. Peter doesn't own the farm; a friend does. But Peter named it. He calls it "Boulderbush Farm." It's well named. Some of the boulders around the fields are as big as the living room of the farmhouse. Harris does some mixed farming, but the reason his friend bought the farm was because of the sugar bush on the property.

It's not a big bush as sugar bushes go. There are a few hundred taps and gravity-fed tubes leading to a sugar shack near the farmhouse. The sap is boiled down to syrup and Harris, a slight but wiry man in his forties, lugs it up in pails to the kitchen of the house. Here's where the similarity to other operators ends. It's here where Harris makes maple syrup barbecue sauce!

He got the idea in a roundabout way. One day he asked his mother to whip up some of the delicious barbecue sauce she'd been making for 30 years. She told him she was busy and he was old enough to make some for himself.

He laughed and told her that it was an impossible dream. But then he began to fool around with his mother's time-honored recipe, using maple syrup instead of honey.

After a few disasters, he got the swing of the thing, and began turning out such varieties as maple mustard and maple blueberry sauce. He was making maple garlic sauce when I saw him. He was using tomato puree, red wine, spice and garlic.

Since he doesn't own the farm, Peter refers to himself as a "resident" and calls his products "Resident's Choice!"

He was distributing it to over 80 outlets at the time, and selling about 10,000 bottles a year. So it appears that he may have a very sweet deal with his syrup and spice and everything nice.

Peter is hard to locate but his products are on sale in some Georgian Bay area outlets.

B.B. and His Fish

Harold, my barber when I'm in the Georgian Bay area, paused for a moment while cutting my hair and said, "Did you know that B.B. Robitaille has left the Tadanac Club and started a fish farm out near Port McNicoll?"

I looked at Harold in surprise. It seemed to me that B.B. (nobody knows his real name), the famous guide and boatbuilder, had lived up the shore among the rugged Thirty Thousand Islands for eons. Maybe even before the Ice Age.

It's true that he had been a year-round camp keeper at the exclusive sportsman's Tadanac Club near Perry Sound for close to 30 years, and the thought of him leaving seemed unnatural somehow. After all, he'd lived up the shore since childhood.

Anyway, Harold gave me directions and the next day I went out to B.B. and his wife Lucille's place. The sign beside the road said "Cedar Creek Farm." I drove up the winding road leading to the farm. It was a scenic route with tall trees shading the road and a bridge crossing over a bubbling creek.

I came upon a big new house; nearby was another building that could have been a workshop of some sort. In the distance were three ponds, and I could see B.B. and Lucille working slowly around the edge of one of the ponds. As I came close, I saw they were feeding fish.

B.B. waved; I hadn't seen him since I'd done a story about him at the Club about five years before. He hadn't changed much. He was still the lean, wiry type I remembered. Not a big man, but as strong as a horse. He's always reminded me of those tough little voyagers I've seen in pictures.

We exchanged greetings and he continued feeding the fish --

rainbow trout in various stages of growth. The fish were leaping out of the water to get their breakfast. "They know who daddy is," laughed Lucille.

I asked him about his radical change of careers. He told me that it had been a dream of his to raise fish, and he'd done considerable research.

Then he led me over to a natural pond. Beneath the surface were fish that could have been two pounds or so.

"These are Arctic char," said B.B., "And as far as I know we're the only ones in Ontario raising them."

I chuckled with glee. "B.B. my friend," I said, "The first time I ever tasted Arctic char was in Greenland when I was up there doing some T.V. shows. And I've never forgotten the experience of eating them. With these fish you'll hit the jackpot!"

B.B. smiled and gazed fondly at the fish. The look on his face was one of sheer enjoyment.

It was quite a switch. B.B. raising fish instead of catching them. And he'd taken to his new career hook, line and sinker.

Getting There

Take Highway 11 north to Orillia. You'll see an overpass. Turn off there onto Highway 12 West. Go about 20 miles. When you reach Waubaushene, watch for Tay Township Concession signs. Go south on Con 5. The fish farm is on the right about a mile down the road.

Kindergolf

❦

J essica Drury took a driver out of her golf bag, teed up at the first hole and let go with a powerful swipe. The ball soared into the air and went about 30 yards, maybe even 40. That doesn't sound like much, but not bad at all when you consider that Jessica was only four years old!

Her partners applauded. There was Marc Burton and Wendy Rozycki, both four. And six-year-old Braden Busher.

"I just love golf," beamed Jessica, her blond hair blowing in the breeze, arms outstretched and blue eyes gazing upward in rapture. "It's so much fun. I just love it."

"You didn't like it last week," snapped Braden. "You said you'd never come here again." Although Braden had joined in applause, Jessica's reaction was too much for him. Jessica glared and began walking down the fairway.

This fearless foursome were members of the Junior Golf League at the Marlwood Club on the outskirts of Wasaga Beach. Along with 85 other members of the League, they'd been taking lessons every Monday during the summer from 34 experienced golfers — all volunteers.

The idea was dreamed up by Debbie Timlock, a Marlwood Club member who was amazed that the League had taken off in a way far beyond her wildest expectations.

"Wasaga business people and the Lions Club helped us financially," she said, "And we were swamped with requests from parents. Now we have a waiting list, I couldn't believe it."

The youngsters use regulation clubs that have been cut down to their size. Ordinarily, they play two holes. I watched some of them on the practice putting green. A volunteer was teaching them. Aside

Bill and members of the Junior Golf League at Wasaga. Everybody enjoyed the game, but concentration was a bit of a problem. Photo: Linda Chernecki.

from actual putting and alignment, they were learning the all-important care of the green, like fixing divots and ball marks.

There was also a practice driving net where the kids can hone their skills. The intermediate group was using it when I wandered over. They ranged in age from seven to 12. Debbie was saying that some of the seven-year-olds are good enough to play with the adult members.

After the lessons, the youngsters got small prizes for things like the longest drive, the fewest putts, and the lowest scores.

But, scores and prizes didn't seem too important to the kids. It was obvious that the fun and love of the game were the big factors.

I suppose you could call the League a form of Kindergolf. Which all goes to show that you're never too young to learn.

Getting There

The golf club road is on the left as you enter Wasaga. They have a great program for youngsters.

Born in a Barn

Were you born in a barn? It's a question familiar to kids who, in their carefree ways, forget to shut doors. Some of us are still lax about such things. When you ask the Bennett family this question, they might hesitate. None of them were actually born in a barn, but they do live in one. It's near the hamlet of Perkinsfield in the Southern Georgian Bay area.

Bob Bennett, a salesman, and his wife, Linda, have always liked barns. They've noticed them in their travels in Canada and the States. They take note of their condition and possible age.

When they saw an old beat-up, dirty and dilapidated barn near Perkinsfield a few years ago, they got an idea. Why not convert the barn into a home? It seemed like an impossible dream at first. But they had plans drawn up, hired a couple of carpenters from the district and, joined by their two teenaged sons, Trevor and David, spent all their spare time on the project.

Gradually, very gradually, the dream came true. Where a thousand laying hens once held sway, there are now comfortable living quarters. What were once a grainery and hayloft are now an attractive living room and dining room. Where a wagon was stored in the old days, there's a modern kitchen. There are four bedrooms and two bathrooms. The rustic quality is still there, but you get a feeling of quiet luxury as you stroll around the place.

It wasn't always that way. Bob kept a photographic record of the process. And in the beginning the barn was a real mess. There are shots of the family cleaning up after pigeons and chickens. It shows the boys replacing some of the boards that had rotted. It was quite a job, but they pulled it off, and it's now a valuable property.

Since none of the Bennetts were born in the barn, they have no real problem with the usual question. Besides, their new dwelling is of an open concept design, and there aren't too many doors to shut anyway -- thanks to the Bennett's conversion.

Getting There

The easiest way to get there is from Penetanguishene, 30 miles north of Barrie. Go to the four corners of the business section. Turn left. You're on Robert Street. Keep going about a mile and at the Shell station, the road curves to the left. You're now on Con. 11 of Tiny Township. Go about a quarter of a mile and you'll see the barn set back from the road. Linda, incidentally, has a stained glass studio there. If you get lost call 705-549-4220.

The Friendly Giant

❦

Charlie Sivell reminds me of the Friendly Giant. He's about six feet tall, which isn't what you'd call giant-size, but when he stands beside the miniatures he makes, he assumes tremendous proportions.

Charlie lives on a side street in Collingwood in a garret-type studio. Scattered around are miniature figures like fairies and gnomes. They're whimsical, mystical little creature that Charlie has carved out of exotic woods. The big ones are about two inches high at the most. Some are as small as a beetle. There are fairies rafting on a leaf, little pixies, and a winged cherub made of Turkish boxwood. Up to four figures can be carved from a small block of boxwood.

Cameraman Rick Dade placed a tiny pixie beside Charlie's boots. Then he panned up to the artist bending over a vice, his hands deftly carving a miniature. The shot worked well with The Friendly Giant idea.

Charlie is a quiet-spoken, personable young man who comes from an artistic family. He's been drawing and painting since childhood, and about fifteen years ago became interested in wood sculpture. From there he moved to carving miniatures. For a while he did odd jobs to make a living, but then his meticulously carved pieces began to get recognition.

Newspaper magnate and art collector Kenneth Thompson bought fifteen pieces. That opened a few doors for Sivell, and now he works full time at his craft. The miniatures sell at four hundred dollars and up, so he's moved out of the starving artist category.

Sivell is well versed in mythology and leans toward the mythical.

"To me there's an ethereal quality about the things I try to produce. They take you out of the mundane and into the world of fantasy," he said. "Even as a child I was intrigued by elves and leprechauns and maybe that just carried over."

He's right. There's a Peter Pan quality in the tiny miniatures. You can see why collectors snap them up. And if you're cramped for space, they sure don't take up much room.

Getting There

Charlie's studio is upstairs at 179 Sixth Street. Go south on the Main street and watch for street signs. Phone 705-444-5884.

Big Bus Company

You wouldn't expect to find the head office of a big bus company in small town Ontario. But although it has offices in four other centres including Toronto, the Penetang Midland Coach Lines still maintains its head office in the Georgian Bay town of Midland. Not only that, it's the oldest family-owned transportation company in North America!

It was started in 1867 as a stage coach operation by Joseph Dubeau, and his great-great-grandsons and their wives still operate it.

There are four hundred and thirty vehicles and six hundred and fifty employees in the big outfit.

In 1992, when Canada was celebrating its 125th Anniversary, the Dubeaus were also celebrating their 125th. And it was quite an affair. The Dubeaus had an old stage coach with a team of horses driven by Laval Dubeau, the president of the firm. Laval was 72 at the time,

and lithe as an athlete. Some of the vehicles are airport buses, and school buses are packed in various parking lots. Hundreds of them.

There's drama in the Dubeau's history. They issued a small magazine on their anniversary. It tells of the trials the family faced in building the transportation company.

At the height of the Great Depression, Joseph's son Albert, who had succeeded him, died at the age of 42. Hard times had taken their toll, and the business was down to two worn buses worth about five hundred dollars each.

Albert's wife, Irene, was determined that her husband's work would not be in vain. With the aid of her four sons -- one of them Laval -- she reorganized the business, plowed profits back into it, and muddled through.

During the difficult times of World War II, she was the only woman in the country to operate a bus line, and she built it into a modest fleet of 14 coaches. After her death, Laval and his five sons took over and expanded the operation to its present strength. It's quite a success story when you consider that it all started with a little old stage coach.

Getting There

The head office of the PMCL is located on Bay Street down by the waterfront in Midland. They have some interesting pictures from the early days.

Blinking Shoes

I've heard there are at least twenty thousand inventors across the country. Few of them ever hit the jackpot. Getting a patent is a lengthy hassle. Getting backing is even worse.

But after many trials, setbacks and disappointments, an inventor who lives in the Huronia district of Southern Georgian Bay finally picked a winner. He marketed a gadget that fits into the soles of shoes and makes a little red light go on and off when you walk. The blinking shoes became a sensation. It wasn't just the safety factor. Kids loved them because they blink and are fun.

We visited the inventor, Nick Shaw, at his home in Cawaja Beach, a few miles from Midland. A self-admitted "eccentric," he was a tall, lean man. His hair was in a pony tail and he was barefoot. He also had a ready smile and a brain like a steel trap. We talked for a while about some of his inventions, aspects of nuclear physics, and the intricacies of getting patents. Half-way through the conversation my mind became fog bound.

But later, down in the cluttered cubby hole of a workshop he calls his "dungeon," I had no trouble comprehending the simple workings of the blinking shoe invention. The device was about the size of a quarter. He explained how he first draws a circuit on a copper clad board, dips the board in acid, and after washing, mounts components such as a battery, resistors and transmitters. Then he puts them all into a mold, glues it all, and inserts the device into the sole of a shoe. Presto! A blinking shoe!

Shaw no longer makes them himself. He sold the idea to L.A. Gear, a big sports company in the States. In just six months, they sold two and a half million pairs of the shoes. They told him it was the fastest selling item they'd ever handled!

Shaw's success didn't come easily, however. He had developed the notion back in 1986. Getting a patent meant going through the inevitable bureaucratic maze. Then he made the rounds of companies he though might be interested. Most of them saw the possibilities, but hesitated. While they were thinking about it, L.A. Gear jumped in and bought the thing outright.

As the inventor, Shaw, of course, gets royalties on the millions of the flashy items that already have been sold. It was a long haul, but now he's walking tall with his blinking shoes.

Nick hit the jackpot. He bought an estate in Costa Rica and moved his young family there.

Carousel Restorer

❦

If you happen to visit Toronto's Centre Island these days, you'll see what appear to be brand new shiny animals going round and round on the carousel. They're not. They're the same old horses, lions and tigers that were made by craftsmen over 80 years ago. But until recently they've been up in the Muskoka town of Huntsville being renovated and restored.

They've been sitting patiently in Al Cochrane's workshop where one by one they've been given new heads, legs, ears or whatever they need and getting coats and coats of paint on their wooden bodies.

The 52 of them make up the only Dentzel carousel of its kind. Dentzel was the first Canadian manufacturer of carousels, and the Dentzel craftsmen became famous the world over.

Al Cochrane is a full time maker and restorer of carousels -- one of the few on the continent. Although he's only in his late thirties, he's a craftsman of the old school. Everything is done by hand, and you won't find a mould or a piece of plastic in the place.

The making of classic carousels was in its heyday at the turn of the century, but the merry-go-round animals crafted right up to the early '20s are now valuable treasures to collectors. For example, the Centre Island carousel is now valued at a cool million and a half dollars!

"There were about 40 people working at the Dentzel factory when this was built," said Al. "It's considered one of the most realistic ever made. Strangely enough, they didn't consider any of these a work of art. To them, it was just a product despite the meticulous detail."

Al has travelled all over the world to research the history of carousels. "It's a form of art that has a very high quality of carving, and one of the few forms that people can actually use," he said.

When he finds the time he will be carving copies based on the Dentzel figures. But when we saw him he was trying to beat a deadline for the completion of the Centre Island job. When he does finish, he will begin another major commission -- carving a completely new carousel. A few of the pieces are already in the process. And you can be sure that all will be done in the tradition of the great craftsmen of yesteryear.

Lucy's Holiday

❧

W hen I was 17, I spent a couple of weeks at a friend's cottage in Bala. And every time I go back, there's a tinge of nostalgia as I recall canoeing on Bala Bay, dancing at Jerry Dunn's Pavilion, summer nights, summer loves, and Japanese lanterns reflecting in the waters.

Bala is still the epitome of all that is Muskoka. It's a beautiful little resort with an air of quiet gentility. An oasis of peace in a hurly-burly world. The Moon River flows under a scenic bridge, there are waterfalls and shady nooks as the river winds past houses and cottages of old-world charm. One of them is a big yellow frame house with a picket fence that's now the Bala museum.

It was started last year by Jack Hutton, an old Press Club buddy of mine when we were Toronto newspapermen. Jack and I would spend many happy hours at the club's piano. "Twenty flying fingers," as Ted Reeve used to quip.

I hadn't seen Jack in years. Then I received a letter telling me about his latest venture -- a museum centered around a holiday in Bala 70 years ago, taken by Lucy Maud Montgomery, author of

Following her holiday in Bala, Lucy Maude Montgomery wrote a novel set in the beautiful Muskoka town.

"Anne of Green Gables." She spent a few weeks there, having her meals at the old house.

The upshot of her visit was a novel called "Blue Castle." The setting was in Bala, in contrast to all of her other novels, which were set in Prince Edward Island.

"It was Bala's best-kept secret," said Jack. "My wife, Linda, discovered the connection, so we bought this place and have had hundreds of people coming and going since we opened."

The couple have acquired some interesting artifacts. Do you remember the rowboat that sank in both the TV and movie versions of "Anne of Green Gables?" Well, the same rowboat is out on the front lawn of the museum.

There's also a vintage piano that was formerly in Bala's old Swastika Hotel. I joined Jack at the piano, and we relived our Press Club days. Some of the songs we played were so old that even Lucy Maud would likely have remembered them.

Getting There

If you've never been to Bala, it will be love at first sight. By the way, there's a beautiful old restored hotel called "The Cranberry" near the lake. Phone the museum at 705-762-5876 to get the hours when it is open. It's not far from the hotel.

The Honey King

❦

Cor Bal was broke. He was living in a borrowed trailer at Honey Harbour on Southern Georgian Bay. He was grubbing away from day to day. There was no stove, and he was reduced to surviving on baby food.

It hadn't always been that way. The tall, lean Netherlands native had been sales manager of a company that hit hard times. When it folded, Cor was out in the cold and deeply in debt.

But Cor was also an entrepreneur. As he sat in the trailer surrounded by about 100 baby food jars, he got an idea. Instead of throwing the jars in the garbage to foul up the environment, he decided to put them to good use.

He did some odd jobs and scraped up a few dollars, rented an empty store in nearby Port McNicoll, bought some honey from a beekeeper in the area, and filled the jars with honey.

He had some labels printed billing himself as "The Honey King." Then he had a retired carpenter make boxes out of scraps of wood to hold the jars of honey. He peddled them as gift packages to a few shops in the area, just to see what would happen. The results were sensational! The honey sold like wild- fire, and Cor realized he had a really sweet deal.

He tied in the idea with environmental programs in schools. He gave the children five cents for each baby food jar they collected and they used the money for their environmental projects. For example, one school was buying three acres of rainforest in Brazil.

I met him three months after he had started the business. Cor had already acquired a panel truck with "The Honey King" painted on the sides, and had 120 customers, many of them in the city.

It was still a one-man operation, using somewhat primitive

When things got tough, entrepreneur Cor Bol had a honey of an idea and put it to work. Photo by Kevin Smith.

equipment. He melted down the granulated honey, poured it into nine big water coolers and filled the jars with nine different flavors of honey. It was a time-consuming job, and he was working 12 hours a day, seven days a week.

He was living in the back room of the store, and the walls were lined with fruit juice bottles which he'd bought from donut shops for a song. They were for his next project -- gift boxes of maple syrup.

Cor bubbled with enthusiasm about the prospects for his venture, and thanks to his honey of an idea, he was busy as a bee. And needless to say, he was no longer limited to eating baby food.

Last I heard, Cor had moved to the city to be closer to most of his customers. He's a great example of enthusiasm and initiative.

Santa Carver

❦

'T was a few nights before Christmas and all through the Simpson house in Stayner not a Santa was stirring. About 20 of them were just sitting there on the shelves. They weren't ruddy-cheeked and chubby. Most of them were stern- looking creatures.

They were about eight inches high, had been carved out of wood by Ray Simpson, and painted by his wife, Pege.

For the Simpsons, it's Christmas all year-round. They're folk artists who create everything from dolphins to duck decoys, but they specialize in Santa carvings. And the distinctive little carvings have become so popular with collectors that they sell them throughout the year.

The Santa carvings are of the historic variety. The stuff of old world myths. One was inspired by a Siberian legend and was known as Father Ice. Another, called Father Christmas, had a rather military look, dressed in a greatcoat and pillbox-type hat. There was a folk Santa of European origin and a Father Christmas from the Victorian period, among others.

None of them were smiling. In most cases, they were serious, even severe. According to legend, some Santas were pretty rough customers. Kris Kringle, for example, a tall, thin type, carried sticks in his bag so parents could use them to spank their children! Compared to old Kris, Scrooge was in the fairy godmother category.

I watched Ray carving a 12-inch-high Santa. It was the largest he had done up to that time. As he chipped away with the chisel, he said, "This is going to be St. Nicholas, the original Santa who was a real person. In the 4th century, he was bishop of Myna, in what is now Turkey, and was noted for his kindness to children."

He went on to say that the name Santa Claus comes from Sinter

Klaas, an affectionate term for St. Nicholas brought to the New World by early Dutch settlers. And the Santa we know so well originated in the last century when Thomas Nasi, an American political cartoonist, drew a happy-looking Santa as an illustration for a story.

I took another look at the carvings. Most of the legendary Santas were lean and mean, thin and grim. So I guess we're lucky to have our own jolly, jelly-bellied happy old Santa Claus.

Getting There

The Simpsons live at 237 Stayner Street. Phone 705-428-2189. They have an extensive knowledge of historical Santas, and the figures are beautifully carved.

Benny's Mine

❦

I'm scribbling this at a corner table in Sunny's restaurant beside The Bon Aire Hotel where I always stay in Timmins. Traffic is whizzing by on Algonquin Blvd., one of the City of Gold's main streets.

Sunny's is a big, busy restaurant, and people are coming and going all the time. Many of them are mining men. There's talk of slopes and stopes, of drilling, of the latest in mining equipment. It's hard to believe that this bustling city was once just a frontier town, albeit a rip-roaring one, where prospectors came to make, and sometimes fritter away fortunes.

One day in 1909, two young men arrived in the area. They weren't miners; they were a couple of barbers from Haileybury who decided to take a fling at prospecting.

Benny Hollinger and Alex Gillies had $145 between them and thought they'd hang around the Porcupine area until their money ran

out. They were advised to stake some claims not far from where I'm now sitting. They tossed a coin to see who would stake the first claim. Benny won the toss, and that claim became the nucleus of the world famous Hollinger Mine, that over a 60- year period produced more than 20 million ounces of gold. That's still a Canadian record.

Hollinger closed 20-odd years ago, but recently what remains of it was turned into a tourist attraction. It's a mini-mine set up ingeniously so visitors can see the real thing on a small scale.

Tour guides take you into a change room where you put on boots, coveralls, hard-hats, lamps and safety belts. Then it's down a ramp into a tunnel, cut through rock years ago, into the underworld of hard rock miners.

The guides are retired miners. The day I was there, Elvin Videto and his partner, Marcel Gosselin, who have 65 years of underground experience between them, led us through the tunnel. They pointed out veins of quartz where gold is hidden, even visible at times.

We walked a few hundred yards to where the two miners have their equipment. We watched Elvin using a hammer drill while Marcel wielded what's called a ''jack leg'' type, as they drilled holes into the rocks. Then a mechanical shovel called a mucking machine lifted the cut rocks into cars. Later they'd be taken out for drying. I've been down in the real thing like the old McIntyre mine, and the process is just the same, but on a larger scale.

Back up on the surface we were taken over to see one of the Hollinger Houses, as they were known. There were 333 identical dwellings, housing 354 families. The one at the tour mine was the last of them and was saved from demolition.

After the tour we wandered around the site looking at old mining equipment. Some of the carts had flower pots in them which added a whimsical touch to the whole thing. As I looked around I was thinking that for a couple of barbers, Benny Hollinger and Alex Gillies had taken a very short cut to fame and fortune.

Getting There

As you go into Timmins on Highway 101, it becomes Algonquin Blvd. Look for Park Avenue. It's close to the downtown area. Turn left and go to Moneta Street. Turn left again and signs will direct you to the mine.

Marble Mine

Twenty years ago, two brothers, Ed and Harvey Blanchard, who were prospecting for gold near Capreol, northeast of Sudbury, came upon a surprising discovery. They found marble! There are only a few deposits of marble in Canada, and this was the first to be discovered in Northern Ontario!

The brothers didn't think much about it at the time. Like most prospectors I've met, they were single-minded. This pair had the lure of gold on their minds.

Besides, even if they did set up a quarry, the marble would have to be sent to Europe for processing. At that time, almost all of the marble used here for buildings and monuments came from Italy, where the valuable stone has always been plentiful.

But things changed. Markets changed. And a few years ago, they took another look at their claims. They considered the possibility of marketing their marble on this continent. The field was almost wide open, so they decided to give it a whirl.

They formed a company, raised funds, and opened five quarries on their property. They began stockpiling marble blocks, and last year acquired extensive, highly sophisticated processing equipment.

One rainy day in May, Ed and Harvy took us out to see one of the quarries. The blackflies were having their annual picnic, and Jenny and I swatted away at them as we clambered over the rock. We've seen various types of mines in the north, but this was a new experience. There were 12 different colors of marble, although it was hard to distinguish them in their natural state. Miners were drilling the hard stone to loosen it up. Nearby was a six-foot belt that looked like a massive chainsaw. We watched as it whirled around, cutting into the rough marble at the rate of 1 1/2 inches a minute. It cut the marble into blocks, each one valued at about $35,000. The blocks were lifted onto trucks and carted off to the processing plant.

We hung around the quarry for a while, then Ed drove us over to see the plant located at Lively, near Sudbury. It was an impressive set-up with giant machinery. There was an 11-foot saw cutting slabs and billets. And on what they called the "tile line," floor and wall tiles were being polished. A few of the finished products were lying around, and they were beautiful.

Ed said there were 30 people employed by the company. His daughter Debra is a knowledgeable Secretary-Treasurer, and Harvey's daughter Belinda is involved in public relations. They put on displays of the product at various trade shows across the continent.

The firm can turn over a million square feet of marble a year. And, although discoveries of gold and base metals in the north country have been common for years, this was a new one. Marble, from Northern Ontario!

Getting There

Call Jarvis Resources. It's in the Sudbury phonebook. They're happy to arrange tours.

The Hole

People who live in the North Bay area call it "The Hole." It's an underground three-story structure 600 feet below the surface of the Canadian Forces Base in North Bay.

A few decades ago when the Cold War was at it's peak, it was built as a station to detect possible enemy aircraft coming into North American airspaces as part of NORAD (North American Aeorspace

Defense Command). It would also provide a headquarters for military and political leaders in the event of a nuclear attack.

The complex was considered top secret. Only those who manned the intricate radar equipment, and 500 or so support staff, were allowed anywhere near it.

Then things changed. The international situation eased. The heat was off. And today, civilians can go down and watch the military personnel who still monitor every inch of airspace around the periphery of Canada. The threat of enemy aircraft is virtually non-existant, but more recently the radar crews have been on the lookout for South American drug smugglers.

We made arrangements with Lieutenant Glen Chamberlain, a public relations officer, to take us down into the famous "hole". The only other one just like it is in Colorado.

We were to meet Glen at his office, but we ran into flak as soon as we arrived at the base. Jenny tried to park close to the admitting gate. Suddenly a big, tough-looking sergeant stormed out of the gate house shouting something about illegal parking. He had a huge black moustache and was wearing a revolver that reminded me of the kind that actor Clint Eastwood hauls out when he threatens the bad guys.

When we explained our purpose and destination, the sergeant barked out rapid directions we couldn't quite follow, and we got out of there as quickly as possible. We got lost in the maze of buildings, but finally found Glen who briefed us on procedure and drove us over to the security check-point, where we had to leave two pieces of identification.

On the surface, all you could see was a grassy knoll, and tucked in beneath it was a round metal opening that appeared to be a water pipe or something. It was the entrance to "The Hole."

There was a military bus waiting for us. We hopped on the bus and drove through the opening into a dingy tunnel which, in 1959, had been cut into precambrian granite. It took three years to build. It was a mile long and our descent was gradual. Eventually we arrived at a clearing where there was a massive 23-ton atomic proof door.

Two husky servicemen opened it for us. It moved back slowly, revealing a long room filled with military personnel, most of them sitting at radar screens with spots scooting across them in various directions.

"These are primarily commercial aircraft," said Glen, pointing to one of the screens. "But we're always watching for anything the least bit suspicious, especially on the coastline of the Maritimes where drug traffickers may try to get through."

Later, we toured the upper floors of the unusual complex. It's a city within a city down in the bowels of the earth. It's totally self sufficient. If necessary, hundreds of people could live there for 30 days at a stretch.

Before we left they gave us lapel pins shaped like mushrooms. The mushroom is their unofficial symbol. It not only represents the well-known mushroom cloud, but also the way mushrooms grow -- in the dark, never seeing the light of day.

Getting There

Call the public relations officer at the Canadian Forces Base in North Bay. They'll likely arrange an appointment for you to visit.

Labour of Love

Every other year Don and Alice Brose get together with a bunch of buddies in the basement of their North Bay home to talk about old times and make sauerkraut.

But it's no small operation. It takes 20 people to do it. They work from early morning to late at night, and when they finish they've made 100 quarts of the famed German dish! In one day!

That seems like an awful lot of sauerkraut, but it all gets eaten.

Don and Alice divide it among their friends and have enough left over to go with their favorite meals for two years. Making the traditional recipe is steeped in family history.

"I remember doing this as a kid," says Don, a musician whose paternal grandfather came to Canada from Germany. "The family would gather in the kitchen of the old country house and make sauerkraut. The house has gone, but the tradition is still alive."

The implements needed have been passed on from father to son. The large barrel where the cabbage ferments has mellowed with age, and the pounders used to crush the shredded cabbage have become rounded at the ends with use.

Don and Alice set aside a date in late October for the sauerkraut session. Once the date is set, they get on the phone and round up their friends, some of whom they've known for over 25 years. When they go into action, everybody has a job to do.

As a first step they lug in 400 pounds of cabbage. They take off the outer leaves, quarter and core before slicing. That's done with a hand-made slicer Don's father put together 60 years ago. When a big tub is finally filled, the sliced cabbage is dumped into the barrel and the pounding with the mallets begins.

This is the toughest part of the job. They pound in pairs, working in 10-minute shifts. I tried it briefly. After about 30 seconds, I nodded to Don to take my mallet. I couldn't keep up with my partner, who was built like a football player.

When the barrel is full, wooden boards are placed across the top, held down by three large rocks. Then it's left to ferment. When the liquid that rises to the top (10 day later) sinks back down, you have sauerkraut ready to bag or bottle.

Although it's a party of sorts, paradoxically they all work like beavers. But in all the years they've been doing it, invariably it's been a rousing success. Never a sour note. Always a labour of love.

It's pretty crowded when Don and his friends begin the annual event, so it's hardly a place to visit. I sat over in a corner watching them at work. Even then I was in the way a couple of times.

Colette's Hacienda

The village of Hamner on the outskirts of Sudbury is one of those typical mining towns that sprung up in the early part of the century when prospectors and mining companies opened Northern Ontario's storehouse of minerals. The buildings are mostly one-story structures, usually painted white and, after all these years, somewhat dilapidated.

But down at the end of the main street you come upon the unexpected. It's a big, magnificent home of an authentic Mexican design, of all things. There's an arch at the entrance to the estate with "Adobe Hacienda" inscribed on it.

To find such a hacienda in a little mining town is surprising enough in itself. But to see it during Christmas season is a rare experience. Every room of the huge home is lavishly decorated. Signs of Christmas cheer are everywhere.

I've seen quite a few houses that are showpieces during the holiday season. But this one has a quality that can be best described as elegant. It looks as if it's been done by professionals. On the contrary, it was all the work of Colette Coutu, whose husband designed and built the lavish dwelling.

Colette has a self-admitted obsession with the yuletide season. A tall, attractive woman, she bubbles with enthusiasm at the mere mention of the holiday.

"I guess I'm a complete nut about Christmas," she laughs. "There's so much love and cheer and it's expressed in the decoration. You see them everywhere you go, but I like to make them rather than buy them. I love to see them come to life."

We were there in November, but Colette has been working on the decorations since mid-summer, as she does every year.

As you enter the home, there's a life-size Santa to greet you in the hallway. Surrounding him are elves and a Father Christmas dressed in a white cloak, along with wreathes and a little snowman. In the sunken atrium, two sculptured Spanish rain gods about 20 feet high gaze down on another tree with another Santa and reindeer. In the living room is still another tree, a manger and choristers. In the family room, Mr. and Mrs. Santa wave greetings beside a miniature Christmas village, and a deer family graces a table in the bathroom.

Everything has been made by Colette in her kitchen, where she's painted a big Santa on one of the windows.

The spell comes over Colette early in August and the hacienda becomes a panorama of Christmas delight. To Colette, love is in the air, wrapped in a big package of yuletide cheer.

Getting There

The house is only open to visitors by appointment. Call Joan Hart at 705-524-9209. She'll be able to give directions and arrange the visit.

Celebrity Socks

A petite go-getter from Sudbury can talk the socks right off you feet. Joan Hart is in the Guinness Book of Records for her collection of "celebrity socks."

She has socks that once graced the tender tootsies of notables ranging from Elvis Presley to Pierre Trudeau. And it's believed she's the only one anywhere to have such an off-beat, off-feet collection. At last count, she had 125 pairs of big-name socks!

Joan is a vivacious woman with a sales personality who's also a translator, artist and world traveller, along with her sales work.

She was born in a railroad station near the Northern Ontario town of Mattawa, and never stopped going. Her parents were French, and she still has an accent that, although very pleasing to the ear, is a bit difficult to decipher at times. And indirectly, it was the accent that got her started on the collection.

In 1970, Joan was headed for Nashville on the same bus as country singer Bill Anderson. She asked him for a couple of songs, but he thought she said socks. Being a good showman, he reached into his bag and gave her an extra pair he was carrying.

Trudeau gave her a pair when they were both travelling on a plane going to Ottawa. She met Sophia Loren while in New York and acquired another pair.

Aside from meeting celebrities in her travels, she began writing to them asking for socks, and her collection got bigger and bigger until she was swamped with socks.

Then the media caught on to it. She was featured in newspapers and on radio and television shows. Before long, the Guinness people got in touch and flew her to England for an interview.

Once again, her accent figured in a further twist of fate. She mentioned on a radio show that she wanted to add to her socks collection, but many of the British listeners through she said "soap", and dozens of various shapes and sizes of soap flooded into the station.

By the time Joan returned to Sudbury, she had become as famous as some of the celebrities she'd met. And on top of everything else, a group of seniors sent her a variety of red Santa Claus socks at Christmas time. Other seniors groups heard about it, and more Santa socks of various designs rolled in. When I saw her recently, she had received over 200 pairs of Santa socks.

Joan says every pair of socks in her collection has a special story, and I can believe it. Whatever the case, amassing such an amazing collection in a somewhat footloose fashion is no mean feat.

Getting There

Joan lives at 1205 Barrydowne Road in Sudbury. Phone 705-524-9209. She's become one of the many friends we've made while travelling the province over the years. I'm sure she'll be happy to show you her collection.

The Phillumenist

Bill Scott and his family live in a cozy cottage on the outskirts of Sudbury. Bill works at Inco, but in his spare time, he's a phillumenist. As usual, the Greeks had a word for it. A rough translation would be "lover of light". And in this case, a phillumenist is a collector of match box covers.

Over the past 40 years, Bill has collected over 30,000 match covers. It's likely the biggest collection in the north. One room in the cottage is packed with albums containing the covers. They're all carefully arranged in alphabetical order. He has a complete album of covers from Australia and New Zealand. Another has a vast assortment from Europe and South America. There are over 3,000 from

Ontario restaurants, many of which Bill collected in his youth while hitchhiking around the province. There's also an album of Canadian Legion covers from the Maritimes to British Columbia.

The album in which I had a more personal interest was the one filled with covers from Ontario towns and villages. There was everything from Allenburg to Zurich. Having travelled the province for so many years, I thought I knew it pretty well, but Bill had covers from little places I didn't know existed!

Then there are offbeat items such as an album shaped like a match box cover, and a cover from the 1939 World's Fair. Apparently there are only 300 in existence. And believe it or not, there's a cover that's a small working calculator.

Bill belongs to the Trans Canada Matchcover Club, based in Hamilton. The members meet two or three times a year to buy, sell and swap covers. I asked him what collectors look for when adding additional covers.

"First of all, the subject matter," said Scott. "Then the age of the cover, the art work, and special qualities. I have one from a Texas hotel advertising rates at a dollar a night. That sort of thing appeals to us."

Bill has been a packrat since childhood. He started collecting sports cards, then stamps and antiques. Eventually he became a phillumenist. And although phillumenism first sparked his interest 40 years ago, his love of his old flame is still burning brightly.

Getting There

Bill is in and out. The best way to get in touch is write to him at Site 10, Box 1, RR 3 Sudbury, Ontario P3E 4H1.

Old Town Gets a Facelift

The lure of gold. Drawn by its siren song, thousands of prospectors swarmed into Northern Ontario in the early 1900s.

They scrambled for claims. Cut their way through rugged bush country in search of the glistening metal that has enthralled fortune-hunters for centuries.

The gold rush opened up the north. Hastily-built towns sprung up. Most had a couple of hotels, a few stores, a claims office and very little else. But they grew and prospered as the gold fields yielded more and more of their hidden treasure.

One of the towns was Schumacher, now located within the boundaries of the sprawling city of Timmins. The town was named after Frederick Schumacher. He wasn't one of those adventurous, hard-bitten types, like Sandy McIntyre and the others who made and sometimes lost fortunes overnight. He was a Danish immigrant who became wealthy buying up claims in the north and other parts of the world. He also became a philanthropist later in life, and backed many projects in the town that bears his name.

In recent years, Schumacher's main street has become somewhat worse for wear. A number of stores have been boarded up. Others are shabby and dilapidated.

But that's all going to change. The old town is getting a facelift. It's being restored. It will look something like it was in the '20s and '30s.

A development committee was organized last year and it has great plans. Joyce Campell was hired to put the plan in action. She's a fast-moving entrepreneur type who's already sparked some improvements. Hannigan's Sports has been painted in its original colours. And the old Medallion Milk Company has been restored. When I was there, it was being used as the committee's offices.

There's a painting hanging on one of the office walls depicting what the committee hopes the town will look like when the restoration is complete. Some of the store will have old-fashioned awnings and the whole main street is bound to be a great tourist

attraction. With the head frame of the famous McIntyre Mine casting its shadow over the town, the whole atmosphere will reflect early mining days.

Joyce introduced me to Louise Smith, who wrote a fascinating book about Frederick Schumacher. Later, I met Frank Zachin, who had a grocery store on the main street in the mid-'20s. He was a dapper, vibrant 83-year-old who bubbled with enthusiasm about the early days. "It was a great town," he beamed. "It was always busy and we had the biggest shopping centre north of Toronto."

At one end of the street is a small monument to Schumacher, who died at the age of 93. Although he settled in the United States, he always had a soft spot in his heart for the little town. No doubt he would be happy that it's being restored and it glory days are to be recaptured.

Getting There

The town is on the outskirts of Timmins, just a block from Highway 101. There should be directional signs. It's quite a project. Joyce's office is easy to find on the main street.

Porcupine Quilling

Porcupines are interesting little creatures. They amble along minding their own business, but as we all know, if threatened the porkies can quickly prove their point.

Yvonne Morrisseau was telling me that the porcupine has been around for over two million years. Yvonne knows a lot about porcupines. She's one of the few experts in the ancient art of traditional quilling, thought to be the oldest form of native art.

Most quilted embroidery you see is done on birchbark. Not

Yvonne's work. She uses moose and deer hides as they did back in the sixth century, long before Europeans arrived on this continent.

I watched her at work in her Sudbury studio. Before any quilling is done, the hides are tanned. It takes time. No chemicals are used; the fibre is softened with deer brains. After being stretched, the hides are washed, and it's quite a trick to wield two sticks to wring them out. It's a tough job.

I was sitting there thinking it wasn't a job for sissies. But Yvonne's no sissy. She's a gutsy woman with a strapping frame, and she handles the hides with ease, which seems somewhat at odds with the delicate intricacies of her artwork.

She showed me how she pulls the quills from a porcupine. The porcupine, like the others she works with, had been the victim of roadkill. Then she began stitching the quills to a hide. There are 28 different kinds of stitches involved. Traditionally, young women of a tribe would learn four stitches a year for seven years.

I roamed off to look at some of her creations that were scattered around the studio. All were impressive, but the one that stood out was a wide hide embroidered with pow-wow cuffs, a hawk hairpiece, a wolf, a bear, a loon and an eagle. As always in native arts, they were symbolic illustrations of the ways and spirituality of the native people.

Yvonne learned the craft while living in Northern Manitoba. She was so apt a student that she became a teacher. She still teaches, and her fondest hope is that her students will help revive traditional methods of quilling.

When teaching, Yvonne totes along an unfinished hide and her mascot named "Spikes". He's a mounted porcupine whose sharp quills are sticking up straight. There's no question "Spikes" would help the students get the feel of the thing.

Getting There

Yvonne lives near the centre of Sudbury. Give her a call at 705-560-8173 and get directions. Her work is magnificent.

Western Ontario

Mennonite Market

❦

The place was packed. Parking lots were full. Thousands of people milled around. It was harvest time, and a cornucopia of fresh fruits and vegetables exuded an aura of abundance.

It was my first visit to the St. Jacobs Farmers' Market. In recent years it's grown to become the biggest agriculturally based market in the province. It's bigger than the famed Kitchener Market, or Toronto's Kensington or St. Lawrence Markets. And on Thursdays and Saturdays, it becomes an agricultural metropolis.

There were over six hundred vendors. Some ran outdoor stalls, others were set up in the four big buildings that make up the complex. It's Mennonite country, and about fifty percent of the vendors were Mennonites. There was a hitching post for their horses and buggies.

Most of the produce had been grown locally. That is, in Waterloo County. And for those looking for specialty foods, it was a panorama of plenty.

There was summer sausage that had been smoked and cured with maple wood. Clad in the traditional Mennonite bonnet, the Amish lady who was selling them had a hard time keeping up with the orders.

In a nearby booth an apple peeling machine was whirling around, and you could watch apple fritters being made right on the spot.

As I walked down the rows of stalls, there were meats, cheeses, crepes, candies, and rosettes. In the flea market you could get anything from crafts to countryside furniture.

I was there on a Thursday when the Ontario Livestock Exchange was having the weekly sale of cattle. Sheila Shanutz, the go-getting young manager of the market, introduced me to Joe Knechtel, who

was watching the sale. Known as "the man with the cowboy hat," Joe was one of the vendors when the market opened thirty-odd years ago. He was eighty-two when I saw him, but he looked about sixty.

"We only had about twenty-five farmers when we started," he said, "And most of the shoppers were from the immediate area. But word got around and city people started to come. And in the last few years the whole thing has taken right off."

I've been to the village of St. Jacobs many times doing various stories. But the huge market seemed to bring together all the elements of Mennonite country. The wonderful simplicity, and the relaxing atmosphere that takes you back to the wholesome eras of bygone days.

Getting There

Go South through the quaint village of St. Jacobs, which is in the Kitchener-Waterloo area on the map. Go about 3 miles south until you come to a stop light. You'll see the market from there.

Scottish Heritage

The swirl of the pipes, the sway of the kilts and the skill and strength of Scottish athletes thrill thousands every year at the Highland Games in Fergus.

The Western Ontario town comes by its Scottish celebrations with honest credentials. It was founded early in the 19th century by two wealthy Scots, Adam Ferguson and James Webster, who sought out other Scots of upstanding character to settle the area. Stone masons soon erected grey limestone buildings that echoed the architecture of their native land.

The Scottish stone masons knew their stuff. Many of the houses they built are still standing. Squat and solid. And nailed on them, small plaques, giving the names and occupations of the original owners.

You can take a walking tour armed with a pamphlet which has historical sketches about each building, and relive the days when the dour Scots carved out a new life in the New World.

We took the tour with Pat Mestern, who knows Fergus and its heritage like the back of her hand. Pat has written three historical novels set in the early days. Apparently, a few eyebrows were raised by some of the locals when they read about the shenanigans of their ancestors. Jenny had read the books, and the two of them were chuckling about the characters.

Some of the houses date back to 1829. I saw where the blacksmith and locksmith lived. The plaque on William Rennie's house said he was a farmer. This appeared to be rather strange, since it was right in the middle of a residential area. But it seems he built his house so his wife and daughter could participate in the social life of the town.

One of the larger houses was occupied by George Ferguson, son of the founder of Fergus. His plaque lists him as "gentleman." He was actually a banker, but in those days banking wasn't considered a respectable business by the Scots.

The oldest house was built by Hugh Black in 1835. He arrived with 13 children and seven wagonloads of furniture. The townsfolk figured he was the one to build the tavern, since no one else had enough chairs.

It's just another of the tidbits of information you get while wandering around a town that positively bristles with history.

Getting There

Pat's office is at the Fergus Chamber of Commerce. Call her as 519-843-5140, and she'll be happy to arrange a tour.

Little Library

❦

Ennotville is a tiny hamlet about eight miles north of Guelph. It has a garage, a restaurant, a few houses, and that's about it.

But there's something that sets Ennotville apart. It has the last library of its kind in the province. And although there are no library cards, no fussy due dates or overdue fines, they haven't lost a book in 145 years!

Mind you, since there's no card catalogue for the 4,000 books -- in fact, no list at all of what's there -- it's pretty hard to tell just what's been going in and out. But trustee Helen Cunningham, who's been visiting the library since childhood and knows it like the back

Librarian Ruth Swan and trustee Helen Cunningham at the entrance of the library. There are no library cards or overdue fines, but they haven't lost a book for over a century.

of her hand, says everything seems to be exactly the way it was when she was a little girl.

The library is one of what were known as community libraries that sprung up in small centres during the last century. Eventually, government grants were withdrawn and the libraries were amalgamated with regional systems. But the Ennotville residents decided to go it alone, and they still run it themselves without a penny in grants.

The librarian, Ruth Swan, lives on a farm next door. She drops around occasionally to dust things off. If you want to get in, you go over to her house and get a key. If Ruth isn't home, you can get the key that's hanging on the wall down at the garage. You go in and get a book, sign a small register with your name and the title and return the key. There's an inconspicuous sign politely asking you to return the book within "a reasonable time."

You don't find the latest best sellers. But you do get the hottest new releases from 1850 to 1940, along with real old-timers like a 205-year-old complete Shakespeare, and topflight articles from an 1860 volume of Harpers.

The library was started by Scottish pioneers who arrived in the district about 1829. For a while, they exchanged their treasured books among themselves. Then in 1847, they built the squat stone building, pooled their books, and the library flourished for several decades.

Today it's needed mostly by students researching the life and times of early Scottish settlers. Other than that, it has a few regular visitors. But its sentimental value is unquestioned.

"I don't think it will ever be abandoned," said Helen Cunningham, leafing through a book she read as a child. "The ghosts would come back and haunt us."

Getting There

Take Highway 8 south from Fergus. In about 5 miles you'll come to Ennotville. Go to the garage and get the key to the library. It's as simple as that.

Local Hero

❧

Becoming a champion is no easy task. But Bob Sinnaeve, Canadian Dart Champion, makes it look that way. He's a friendly, easy-going man in his early '40s, who strolls up to a dart board, adjusts his horn-rimmed glasses and almost casually shoots darts with a precision that thrills thousands of applauding spectators at tournaments the world over.

Yet Bob is a country boy who lives in the village of Langton in Southwestern Ontario. It's a friendly little place on Highway 59, a stretch of road that meanders down toward Lake Erie. He's not just Canada's best at the game. Sinnaeve has been ranked in the first four among the world's top professionals. He travels to faraway places like Japan, Australia, and of course, England, where darts is a major sport. Wherever he goes, he's quite a celebrity on the circuit.

And just as Parry Sound has a sign on the highway as you enter the town which reads "Home of Bobby Orr," and Brantford has "Home of Wayne Gretzky," Langton has one proudly proclaiming it to be "Home of Bob Sinnaeve."

Bob's house is diagonally across the road from the back of the sign. It's a big old home. Down in the recreation room there's a dart board where the champ works out occasionally. Some of his trophies are standing on a mantlepiece, and others are hung around the room. There are also citations from the federal and provincial governments for community service, since Sinnaeve often visits schools throughout the country to teach the game to young children. Most of his trophies, however, are stored away in four large packing cases.

When I saw him, he had just returned from Japan and was spending some time with his wife Judy and their children before taking off on a 29-stop promotional tour across the country.

I asked him if he still enjoys the sport despite 16 years of professional competition. "I like it, but not as much as I used to," he said.
"The younger players take the game too seriously these days.
They're money mad and seem to forget that primarily it's supposed
to be a game for enjoyment. To me, the money is secondary."

That may be the one reason why Bob hasn't become a full-time
pro. He has a small heating business, a young family and is com-
munity-minded. And besides, around Langton he's not the big-time
darts celebrity. He's just plain old Bob, and that's the way he likes it.

Getting There

*Langton is south of Tilsonburg on Highway 58. (It's also the hometown of
global anchor Mike Anscombe) You may have noticed that early in 1994, John Part
of Oshawa became world champion in darts. He's a former doubles partner of
Bob's.*

Big Time in Miniature

❦

Maurice Wideman is a stocky man with a chubby face, lots of white hair, and a jovial personality. With a beard and red suit he'd make a great Santa Claus. And in a way, he has a lot in common with old St. Nick. He has a workshop behind his home in the Western Ontario village of Delhi. And he's a craftsman who creates miniature heritage buildings that would make some collectors jump for joy if they got them as gifts.

Wideman is a sculptor who is considered one of the most gifted professionals in the trade. For the past few years he's been specializing in American heritage buildings. The big market for them, of course, is south of the border.

We watched him as he was completing a model of Paul Revere's house. He crafts in clay. It's meticulous, detailed work. Every shingle on the house had to be carved separately. His tools are simply things he makes himself from odds and ends like old razor blades and pot scrubbers.

So far, there are close to 50 pieces in the collection. They include the Railroad Inn, which features an old hotel with a locomotive standing beside it. The Mississippi Belle is an old-time riverboat; with its 144 windows it was a real challenge. And there's a bandstand of the type Wideman uses as a platform when giving lectures and demonstrations during his frequent tours through the United States.

The intriguing little buildings are made in their entirety at the workshop. And when I saw him he was just starting a line of native Canadian miniatures.

I asked Maurice how he happened to become specifically interested in American heritage buildings. "Ironically, the idea was sug-

Maurice Wideman makes remarkable miniature heritage buildings, and is considered the best in the business.

gested by an English company headed by John Hine," he laughed. "He saw some of my work and liked it. So I took my family over to England for a year and we worked out the details," said Wideman. "My son picked up an English accent after starting school there," he added with a chuckle.

He has a great sense of humor. Sometimes, when people ask him what he does for a living, he tells them he's "in construction." And he is. He's a bricklayer, a roofer, and puts on siding. Not in a big way, of course. But he's big time in his own small world.

Getting There

Delhi is south of Brantford on the road map. Maurice lives at 121 Wellington Street. It's at the corner of Queen and Wellington. Phone 519-582-2110. You'll find his famed miniatures intriguing.

Frank's Garden

By all the laws of nature, Frank Schaefer's garden shouldn't exist at all. Not in Ontario's climate anyway.

Frank's place is located on a pleasant residential street in Woodhouse Acres, just east of Port Dover. As you drive along the street, you see tidy houses with well-kept lawns. Then suddenly, there's a jungle out there! Trees, shrubs, plants and unfamiliar vines rise up, and you wonder if you're on some sort of safari.

If you take a closer look you see a driveway, and set back amid the lush foliage is an attractive home where Frank and his wife Sylvia live. It's surrounded by over 300 exotic trees and plants. Although their half-acre of land looks a bit like a forested area in the tropics, it's right on Lake Erie's north shore!

There's pampas grass, a monkey puzzle tree, sassafras, a silk tree, an umbrella magnolia with beautiful blossoms, along with

Australian tree ferns set in a verdant grotto. It's a botanical showplace!

The spread of greenery is heavily hedged and wind-sheltered by evergreens of the broad-leafed variety. There are Himalayan pines, weeping willows and Japanese umbrella trees, among others.

Frank is a stocky man with a weatherbeaten look, who reels off the scientific names of his plants and trees with the greatest of ease. Born on a farm in his native Germany, he studied agriculture, but had absolutely no horticulture experience when he started the garden 30 years ago.

At first he planted the same type of garden his neighbors had. Then he got the notion he'd like to grow trees of a tropical nature. He talked to a few experts. They smiled. They told him he was barking up the wrong tree. They said it couldn't be done in Ontario.

"They underestimated the possibilities," said Frank, as we poked around the winding paths. "I had the soil and location going for me. This is clay soil with a layer of sand, and the average temperature is higher than in most parts of Ontario."

There are at least 50 plants in the garden the experts said were impossible to grow in our climate. But when someone tells Frank he can't grow something, it's like throwing down the gauntlet. He can't resist a challenge. And when he gets it, he's off and running to add another impossible dream to his botanical oasis.

Getting There

Frank lives on Lakeview Avenue, the first street on the left as you enter Port Dover on Highway 6. Go about 200 yards and you'll see the foliage.

Dave and Seaweed

❦

I'd been there before, and the old seadog was just where I expected him to be. Dave Stone, the Beachcomber of Long Point, was ambling along the Lake Erie shoreline with his dog Seaweed tagging along behind him.

For close to half a century the colourful sailor, diver and historian has covered the north shore, searching for marine artifacts washed up on the beach near Long point. They're the remains of the many ships asleep in the deep of the Point, that sliver of a sandpit that juts out into the lake.

Stone is an expert on Ghostships, as they're called. An experienced diver, he's gone down to examine hundreds of the wrecks that were claimed, mostly late in the last century, by the treacherous stretch of the lake known as the "Quandrangle."

A few years ago he wrote a book subtitled "Last Port of Call", giving a history and innumerable details about the Ghostships. I wrote a foreword for the book, saying I was surprised when I first met the Beachcomber. To me, he didn't fit the image of an old salt at all. He looked more like Fred Astaire, with the same mild-mannered charm, and a mind as nimble as Astaire's tapping shoes.

For a while we lost touch. But Stone resurfaced in 1991 during the controversy surrounding the steamer "Atlantic". The wreck had been discovered by Mike Fletcher, a young diver from Port Dover. But a Yankee group claimed that, although the ship had gone down in Canadian waters, it had been an American vessel and belonged to them for salvage. They put a marker over it and a U.S. flag.

The mild-mannered Stone suddenly changed into a firebrand. He hopped into his boat, went out to confront a team of American divers who happened to be at the site, pulled up the marker and flag, and threw them into the water!

Then last year the old seadog dropped something of a marine bombshell. He and another expert on the lake, David Frew of Pennsylvania, collaborated to write a book called "The Lake Erie Quadrangle." In it, they claimed the Quadrangle was more dangerous than the Bermuda Triangle!

I was curious and went down to see Dave again to get a few facts. I wasn't disappointed. He brought out a chart comparing the two infamous waters.

"The Bermuda Triangle stretches for 14,000 square miles and has had 112 disasters," he explained, "While the Lake Erie Quadrangle goes for just 2,000 square miles but has had 420 marine disasters. That makes it 21 times more dangerous. In fact, it's the most dangerous spot anywhere."

I dashed off a TV script, and Rick took pictures of Dave and Seaweed walking along the beach. Although he's in his '70s and is one of the oldest divers in the country, I have a feeling the Beachcomber will be wandering the waterfront for a long while yet, in constant search for the sunken secrets of our maritime history.

Getting There

During the spring and summer Dave is at 23 Beach Street in Long Point, but his mailing address is Port Rowan P.O. Phone 519-586-2870. During the winter he's at his home in Tugersole. Phone 519-485-1423.

The Bag Lady

I've seen the odd bag lady on city streets pushing a cart containing all her worldly possessions. But I never expected to get a letter from one. Especially one who lives in the tiny community of Otterville in Southwestern Ontario. Moreover, she suggested I visit the village to see its historic landmarks! It takes a lengthy stretch of the imagination to visualize any bag lady who has even the slightest inclination to promote historic sites.

Anyway, I went to Otterville one spring morning to meet the small-town bag lady. But she didn't fit the usual mould at all. She wasn't dressed in old clothes and she wasn't pushing a cart. She was a vibrant, attractive 70-year-old named Lorraine Downing. Until his death a few years ago, her husband was the village doctor.

"The Bag Lady" moniker is a trade name she uses to tag on the bags and purses she makes by hand. The profits from selling them go to the South Norwich Society to support its ongoing restoration project. Lorraine is also one of the volunteer guides who take people around to see sites.

We strolled along the main street, past tasteful shops, and down a hill to Otter Creek, a river that runs through the centre of the village. There's a dam and scenic waterfall, which supplies water power for an old mill built in 1845. It's believed to be one of the oldest, continuously-operating water- powered mills in Canada. The conversion to metric brought business to a standstill, but it's kept in top-flight condition.

At the west end of the village is another historic gem. It's a restored octagonal house built in 1861 and is now used as an adult community centre.

Among other points of interest is a gothic-style church, an old bank and a privately-owned motorcycle collection. A railway station from 1875 is in the process of restoration.

Later, we walked over to the bungalow where Lorraine lives so I could see the bags she makes. On the way she pointed to a large mansion atop a hill. "That's now a residence for seniors," said Lorraine. "It was our home for many years and where we raised our family." I was thinking it was a pretty posh place for a bag lady.

The bags themselves are made of upholstery or tapestry materials and vary from tote bags to cheque book holders. It takes an average of six hours to design and sew each bag.

"After expenses I make about as much as a parking metre does," laughed the bag lady. "But every little bit helps the restoration fund."

I waved goodbye to Lorraine as I started to drive back to the highway, but stopped along the way to take another look at the waterfall and the mill. It was indeed a village of quiet, natural beauty with a wealth of history. Just as the bag lady had said in her letter.

Getting There

Take Highway 3 west to Delhi(see road map). At Delhi, take Highway 59 north. You'll see a sign directing you to Otterville. Everybody knows the Bag Lady. They'll direct you.

The Backus Mill

Nestled beside a quiet stream and surrounded by a picturesque rolling landscape, the 200-year-old John Backus Mill, the longest-operating grist mill in the province, stands as a memory of an earlier era. The surrounding terrain of woodlands and wetlands is now a conservation area near famed Long Point which juts out into Lake Erie, and it's visited by thousands of tourists and schoolchildren annually. But in recent years something new was added. An Education Centre was opened near the mill, and it's a real winner!

When we were there, some of the designers were putting the finishing touches on a wildlife gallery in the foyer of the building. It's a magnificent display that was put together by artists, artisans and workmen who live in the district. A huge mural map of Long Point forms a backdrop for the simulated flora, fauna and wetlands.

In the foreground is a tree that looks so real you expect to see a leaf drop from it at any moment. The tree, along with many other features in the display, was made by Vision and Design, a company located near the neighboring town of Simcoe.

There's an interpretive study of the area's sand dunes and the importance of preserving grasses to hold them. Perhaps the most striking of all is the waterfowl display. It shows marshlands with realistic looking mallards and bluebills among others.

The driving force behind the creation of the centre has been conservation authority Bill Courtnage. I didn't get a chance to meet him, but apparently he's steered the project through countless meetings, and overcame objections and reluctance of some other members to go through with it. Historian and naturalist Harry Barrett was roaming around the complex. I've known Harry for quite a while and knew he'd had a long-standing interest in the project. His baby has been the waterfowl display. Harry took us into an adjacent workshop where Bill Gunn was hammering away. Bill has been doing carpentry work for the centre for the past three years. He's been one of the volunteers who don't charge a penny for their work. Near the workshop is a classroom where children learn firsthand of the natural world around them.

But to me, the main attraction is still the mill itself. It's a beautiful, old wooden structure and goes full tilt during the summer months. By the way, the family's original name was "Backhouse." But John's wife, who became a lady of some standing in the community, thought the name was undignified, so John changed it to Backus. I'll bet every kid who lives on Lake Erie's north shore knows that tidbit of history.

Getting There

Take Highway 58 south from Tiltsonburg to Port Rowan on Lake Erie's north shore. The Backus Mill is on the outskirts. Look for the directional signs.

Family of Newsies

❧

Forty years ago, Linda Thompson started a paper route. When she outgrew it, her younger sister Diane took over. When she was ready to give it up, a still younger sister inherited it, and so on down the line until finally the tenth child in the family called it quits.

But that's only the beginning of the story. Ada Thompson, the mother of the string of newsies, picked up the torch and began walking the three-mile route, delivering the paper six days a week. All this took place in the fishing village of Port Dover on Lake Erie's north shore, where Ada now takes The Simcoe Reformer, The Brantford Expositor, and The Hamilton Spectator to about a hundred customers.

She's crowding 70 and is as fit as a fiddle. She strides along with pep, power and purpose through a system of alleys and improvised pathways she has mapped out throughout the Port Dover neighbourhoods. Even at that, it takes her five hours to complete the route. One reason is she takes about 20 papers from her house and, after delivering them, goes back home to get another bundle. Another is that she stops to talk to some of her customers, especially those who live alone.

Stan Morris, who edits Port Dover's weekly paper, thinks the Thompson family has established a record for continuous delivery.

"I've never heard of a family who have kept up such a lengthy relay among carriers," he said. "I've checked around and nobody else has either. As far as I can gather, it's a record."

On one occasion, the Spectator honored the 10 Thompson newsies and Ada has a photo and write-up of the event. Later, the paper did a lengthy feature about their mom.

When Linda started the route, papers cost thirty cents a week for daily delivery. Of course, that was 40 years ago. Meanwhile, Ada has no thought of giving it up. She's a carrier who'll continue to carry on.

If you're visiting Port Dover, maybe you'll see Ada on her rounds.

Ernie's Peanuts

❦

The village of Vittoria, west of Simcoe, isn't very big, but at one time is was the capital of the district. Now it's the self-styled Peanut Capital of Canada.

That's because Ernie Racz, a pioneer peanut farmer in Canada, operates the Kernal Peanut plant on the outskirts of the village, and farms over 120 acres of Valencia peanuts.

Originally, Ernie's father had a very profitable tobacco farm on the site, but by the time Ernie was ready to take over, the market for tobacco had dwindled.

Ernie and his wife, Nancy, wanted to save the farm at any cost. They knew that Jim Picard, who farmed a few miles down the road, had converted to peanuts, and they knew the sandy loam and climatic conditions were right. They also knew it was a gamble. They needed special equipment, since harvesters used in the States weren't suitable for Ontario.

They started from scratch, built a giant harvester and invested in processing equipment to shell, sort and so on, as well as to make peanut butter. There were packaging, distribution and promotional hurdles that they managed to muddle though.

Ernie began to realize, as he puts it, "You have to add value to your product to survive." The answer was variety, and they began to make almond butter, cashew butter and sunflower butter along with their regular peanut butter.

They brought in a partner to distribute the new line, and before long the products were going to health food stores across the country.

I watched employees making almond butter. The almonds (imported) went from a conveyer to a hopper, and after grinding, the resulting almond butter was pumped into jars and packed in boxes. In an adjacent warehouse, boxes were stacked to the ceiling.

They turn out a quarter of a million pounds of almond butter a year. They also fill you full of information. For example, the peanut isn't a nut at all. It's a legume, like a bean. It's cholesterol-free and packed with protein. As their slogan says, Nuttin' But the Best.

Getting There

Take Highway 24 south from Simcoe. Go about 5 miles and you'll see Ernie's sign on the right hand side of the road.

Wooden Wonders

❦

It all happened by accident," said Janet Morton as she put the finishing touches on a rocking horse she'd made.

She was talking about the woodworking shop she and her husband have at the four corners in Caledonia.

The couple have a farm on the outskirts of the town. They couldn't afford to spend much on furniture and, when one of the children accidentally broke a bed they'd just bought, it was the last straw.

Brad's hobby was woodworking, so he taught Janet a few tricks of the trade and the two of them began making furniture for their own use.

That was 10 years ago. Today, Morton's Furniture and Woodworking is a place of wooden wonders. There are beautiful cabinets, bookcases and other small items like trucks, bulldozers, doll high chairs and whatnot.

But what really sets the shop apart are the rockers. Along with the horses, there are ponies, cows, bulls, donkeys and even camels. Janet designed the rockers and still makes most of them herself.

"We can't keep up with the demand," she says. "People from as far away as Chicago and the Yukon have bought them, and tourists from other countries send them home as gifts."

When we were there, Brad had just finished making a replica of a 1920 wooden delivery truck. It was a beauty -- a pet project that had taken three years to complete.

Although they sometimes use exotic woods for special jobs, the Mortons work mostly in oak and pine, and the animals are always carved in pine because it's a light wood which makes it easier for children to handle.

They don't have too much time to milk the cows anymore. They're always on the move at the shop and have two employees to help them.

They have all sorts of custom work, but what made their name was the rocking horse idea. They think that the rockers have been sent to every country in the world. So the Mortons are justifiably proud of their Rocking Horse Winners.

Getting There

You can't miss Morton's. It's a great little shop. Caledonia, by the way, is on Highway 6, south of Hamilton.

The Gentle Barbarian

When I first saw Alex Godden, I thought he was a Norseman. The long, fair hair that framed his rugged features brought visions of the marauding Eric the Red or some such rogue. But Godden is nothing of the sort. He's a mild-mannered artist who lives in a converted schoolhouse built in 1893. It's set in among huge trees near the hamlet of Renton, just east of Simcoe.

I watched Alex standing at his easel painting a floral design. It was delicate work, his busy hands gently adding touches to the design. But those same hands also built the big, iron woodstove sitting in a corner of the high-ceiling living room. And the same hands pound, shape and fit stainless steel into art that's seen in gardens, museums and galleries, mostly around Southwestern Ontario. Although an accomplished painter, it's the metal sculptures that impress art lovers.

I first saw Godden's work at the Cruise estate in Marburg. Dr. Jim Cruise, formerly director of the Royal Ontario Museum, has a stately blue heron standing beside a pond near the historic Cruise homestead. Author and historian Harry Barrett, who lives nearby, has a kingfisher made by Alex. And I saw a huge eagle of his in the MacAdam Gallery in Port Dover. The price was a hefty 15 thousand dollars. It had a wing span of six feet and had hundreds of feathers of steel.

All of these magnificent pieces, and the many which have been created over the past decade, were crafted in a workshop behind the old school house. Alex took me out there. It could have been a blacksmith shop. There were a forge and various types of hammers. But there were also welders and drills.

Godden was working on a piece at the time that reflected my first impressions of him. There was a certain wildness to it. He told me it was his concept of a barbarian -- a Vandal, or perhaps a Goth. He showed me the sketches he had made before starting the work. "It allows me to release my aggressions," he laughed. I stood back as he welded a metal strip to the frame.

I asked how long it usually took him to make one of the sculptures. "I haven't the slightest idea," he said. "If you start wondering about time it spoils your thinking."

Later we wandered out to the garden. There were a variety of plants, bushes and flowers and a pond in the centre. Alex had designed and planted it himself.

I found it interesting that this big, rugged-looking man had so many artistic facets. I mentioned it to him. "Creative work keeps me going," he smiled, "after all, it's the spice of life."

Getting There

Alex's studio is about 3 miles east of Simcoe on Highway 3. There's a sign outside saying "Sculpture". His mailing address is RR #5 Simcoe, Ontario. Phone 519-428-1655.

Summer Gardens

I have fond memories of the dance halls of yesteryear when we'd while away the hours, perhaps in an aura of romance, or with youthful exuberant joy pumped up by the big beat of the big bands of the day.

There was Jerry Dunn's Pavilion in Bala, the Brant Inn near Hamilton, the huge pavilion in Port Stanley and the Summer Gardens in Port Dover.

The Summer Gardens was in its heyday during the twenties and thirties, and the memory lingers on in murals at Knechtel's.

Most of them have disappeared. But in Port Dover, memories of the Summer Gardens still remain, and of Don Ivey, the man who ran it for years, as did his father before him.

Fred Knechtel's big restaurant overlooking Lake Erie's shore now stands beside the area where the Summer Gardens was located before it burned to the ground in 1979. One wall of the restaurant is covered with a huge mural. It shows Don sitting beside the bandstand dressed in his characteristic white suit and red bow tie. The mural extends to show people in bathing suits on the sandy beach. It's a scene that somehow seems to reflect a combination of eras.

Port Dover is a heritage-conscious village. You get the impression that the residents are always commemorating something. So it was quite natural they'd organize a Summer Gardens Reunion. Early in 1992, they got the ball rolling. The Lighthouse Theatre people had a play written about Don and his dance hall. It's a top-flight professional company and the play was a real winner.

Then they hired a big band and had a dance at the community centre. They had turnstiles and it was a "10 cents a dance" affair. The actor who had played the part of Don in the play kept an eye on things. Don was very fussy about dress and decorum and the reunion guests made sure they didn't step out of line.

I did a T.V. item about the event. I talked to Jamie Ivey, Don's son, who told me that his grandfather started the gardens back in 1921. And Lois Snider was there. Lois is now one of Port Dover's best known citizens, but in the old days she was the hat check girl.

It was a reunion filled with nostalgia. A panorama of memories depicting the life and times of the fabled Don Ivey and his Summer Gardens.

Getting There

Port Dover is on Lake Erie's north shore, south of Brantford. Knechtel's is located on the waterfront beside the Erie Beach Hotel where we always stay. You'll like the mural, along with the many photos from yesteryear of the Port and its people. It's a picturesque village - a bit of the maritime right in Ontario.

Easter Egg Chickens

❦

You may have heard of chickens that lay colored eggs. They're rare birds. You don't find them in any old barnyard. Commonly known as Easter Egg Chickens, they're of the Araucanian breed, named after the Araucanian Indian, an early South American tribe. And they lay eggs in shades of gold, green and purple.

I'd heard that Dr. James Cruise was raising some of the unusual birds at his farm in the hamlet of Marburg, a few miles from Port

Dover. Dr. Cruise (call me "Jim") is one of the area's most distinguished citizens.

After he retired as the director of the Royal Ontario Museum, he returned to the homestead where his family has farmed for generations. He still farms in a small way, but has also spent much of his time turning the big, rambling farmhouse into a magnificent example of early Canadiana. His barnyard "friends" as he calls them include a llama, a few goats, sheep and the chickens.

He had about 45 hens and a few colorful roosters the day I saw him. What distinguishes the birds are their tuft-like whiskers which grow out from the sides of their heads. And, of course, the colored eggs. Some of the birds are rumpless, others have tails like the usual chickens we see.

Jim got his first pair from Chile. It's unknown where the genes for the eggshells came from. Jim thinks they may have occurred through cross- breeding with a native South American bird known as the tinamou, which lays strongly colored eggs.

I mentioned that I've occasionally seen farmers at Fall Fairs displaying colored eggs that presumably came from their chickens.

"Don't let them fool you," smiled Jim. "There are only a few breeders of these chickens in Canada. What the farmers have done is dye the eggs with food coloring."

Jim gave me a dozen colored eggs as I was leaving. I had one for breakfast the next day and enjoyed it. The flavor seemed more pronounced than in the average egg.

Maybe I'll go back and get some more around Easter. But it doesn't matter when you go. Jim has Easter eggs all year long.

Getting There

Jim lives near the village of Marsburg on the outskirts of Port Dover. From Dover go east on Chapman Street. It winds around and becomes Cockshutt Road. Turn right at Lynn Valley Road. Go about 2 miles. There's a sign outside the estate. Phone first. The number is in the Port Dover section of the phone book.

Computer Composer

Hermann Lorenz is a retired industrial mechanic who lives in the village of Burford, a few miles west of Brantford. He loves classical music. He can read the music, but he can't play it. He says he hasn't the hands for it, and his aptitudes are mathematical and mechanical rather than musical.

However, after considerable practice, he managed to learn to play the opening bars of Beethoven's "Moonlight Sonata" on his Yamaha Clavinova, a versatile keyboard instrument. To a musician, the opening phrases of the Sonata are relatively simple. After that, it's more complex.

I listened as Hermann played what he knew of the melodic masterpiece. But when he came to the more difficult part he threw up his hands in mock despair. "That's it," he shouted. "That's all I know. After that I'm a dead duck!"

But then he reached over to a computer sitting beside the Clavinova, pressed a few keys and Presto! The remainder of the Sonata boomed out from the Clavinova through stereo speakers.

There's nothing too unusual about that. It could have been prerecorded. But here's the twist: Methodically reading from the musical score, Lorenz had punched the whole Sonata into the computer, every note, the length of the note, the velocity, was entered one by one. Through a sophisticated process, all of it was relayed from the IBM compatible computer to the Clavinova. Even more remarkable is that Hermann has put together over 50 classical selections in this way. His most massive job was transposing Beethoven's 5th Symphony in its entirety. Working six hours a day, it took him four months to complete the task!

Needless to say, he works at a snail's pace. Note by note, every detail of the lengthy scores are entered into the computer. When he completes the selection, he retains it on a floppy disk. Over the years, he's written out more than 1,500 individual bars of music from his large collection of classical scores.

So, although he's not on the podium, this maestro can produce the world's great music as the man behind the scenes. He may not be able to play, but he sure knows the score.

Mainly Because of the Heat

❦

P ort Ryerse is a place of quiet charm, nestled in along Lake Erie's north shore. There's a little white church and a general store and some nice houses. That's about all there is on the main street.

But up on a hill overlooking the village is a big greenhouse complex that was the first in the country to use "bio-mass" heating in growing greenhouse vegetables. That's using natural substances like corn cobs, peanut shells, sawdust and such to heat the 28,000 square feet under glass.

Farmer Dave Smith, of what's called Ryerse Farm Market, began using organic fuel over 10 years ago. Since then, hundreds of agricultural students have come to see it in action.

Smith doesn't have any hi-tech equipment. The heating machinery was made right at the farm. If something goes wrong, there's no service company to fix it. He has to figure it out himself. It looks somewhat primitive but it sure works.

The organic material gathered for fuels is first screened to remove rocks and so forth. Then it goes to a revolving hopper which creates a mass that's taken by an elevator over to a fiery furnace. The heat goes to a large boiler and the steam pressured into pipes that run throughout the hot houses.

The vegetables, mostly tomatoes and lettuce, are grown hydroponically. That is, in water. There's not a scrap of earth in the whole complex. The tomatoes are red, round and juicy, and there's a greenhouse of what Dave calls "living lettuce". It's pulled up from the watery bed, roots and all, put in packages, shipped and will stay fresh for nine days.

Dave began recycling for heat for several reasons.

"Farmers traditionally have had to be very efficient and conscious of the environment because it's their livelihood," he said. "And it makes sense that a source of heat comes from a renewable resource. Besides, when you operate year-round as we do, you have to think of fuel economy."

Dave took us into one greenhouse he calls his "foolin' around house." It's experimental. When we were there, he was trying to grow beans using hydroponic methods.

The students who visit are interested in all of the farm's experimental features. "But let's face it," smiles David, "It's mainly because of the heat."

Getting There

Go south from the town of Port Simcoe on Highway 24. Ryerse is just a few miles from Simcoe. You'll see a road sign on the south side of 24 directing you to the village. The Ryerse Farm Market is on top of the hill.

The Great Law

Chief Jake Thomas had been reciting The Great Law six hours a day for nine days! He had no notes, and although in his seventies, his voice remained strong and resonant.

It was an historic occasion -- the first time The Great Law of Peace of the Iroquois Confederacy had been recited in English. Chief Thomas was the logical choice to do it. He's a highly respected traditional chief, historian and educator who speaks five languages.

The event took place at the Iroquois Institute on the Six Nations Reserve near Brantford. The Institute is an organization devoted to the preservation of native culture.

Two huge tents had been set up and hundreds were listening intently to the Chief's recitation and commentary. Colourful figures from many tribes were in attendance. They had come from various parts of Canada and the United States.

My guide was a brilliant, knowledgeable, articulate young man named Wray Anderson. He had been living in California attending university there, but had returned to his roots and had joined the staff of the Institute.

Although I was not unacquainted with native philosophy and spirituality, my knowledge was increased tenfold after spending a few hours with Wray. He filled me in on some historical data as well. He told me that native heritage can be traced back to the Mayan Civilization, and that the laws and customs as set down in The Great Law of the Six Nations form the basis for democracy as we know it.

Contrary to the notions we were given in textbooks and movies, native people were far from being "savages" who had to be "civilized." They had a highly developed social order which was disrupted after the arrival of the Europeans.

What surprised me most was the similarity between The Great Law and the Constitution of the United States. Wray placed abbreviated printed versions of the two side by side. Either deliberately or by chance, the two had much in common. There was no question that the basic principles were much the same.

To those assembled at the site, the reading of The Great Law in English was a world event. Wray explained that it was a compromise, since not too many these days understand their native tongue.

It was the final day of the reading. Before I left I stood at the entrance of the tent and listened. After nine days the old chief was still going strong.

Getting There

Take Highway 6 south from Hamilton. You'll go through Hagersville and Caledonia. A few miles out of Caledonia there's a highway sign directing you to the Reserve. The Institute is a short distance down the road on the right hand side.

Creative Carvers

In many ways the village of Ohsweken on the Six Nations Reserve near Brantford combines two worlds. There's a modern shopping centre with a native decor, a community radio station, a newspaper and a modern band office. Yet everywhere native symbols and native ways are in evidence.

There are many artists and craftspeople in the village. I've known several of them over the years, including potters Steve and Leigh Smith who have become recognized internationally for their magnificent pottery.

It was Steve and Leigh who told me about a father and son team of carvers in wood and stone. They have a small workshop near the four corners in the centre of the village, and their work has overtones of the spirituality so characteristic of native art.

The father, Garfield Jonathan, was injured in an accident some years ago and began carving as a hobby. His son, Kelly, who showed artistic talent in childhood, studied fine art and later joined his dad as a carver, although he also does striking paintings.

The tools they use vary from knives and power saws to dental instruments. Garfield showed me an intricate carving of a bear catching a fish. He had made it from a huge tree knot. But he downplayed his own work, saying that Kelly had the real talent in the family.

And apparently Kelly's carvings and paintings have caused quite a stir among collectors. The ideas for his paintings come from his dreams, while those for the carvings are all drawn from native legends. One carving called "Grandmother's Gift" depicts an older woman holding out a child to its parents after one of its daily visits to her. The piece was on its way to Japan, having been sold for $10,000. Another is called "Thunder Cloud." According to legend, thunder is the voice of grandfathers.

Kelly can tell you all sorts of nature myths and legends. "I learn them from the elders," he said. "I'm always on the lookout for our older people. The stories are passed down from one generation to another."

So the father's hobby became the son's career. Both father and son are very proud of their ancient heritage and, like the elders, are using their talents to pass it on to future generations.

Getting There

There are two ways to get to the Six Nations. See "The Great Law" story for the Highway 6 route. If you're going from Brantford take 24 south to Sourspring Road and turn left. When you get to the 4 corners of the village, check at the Village Inn Restaurant. They'll tell you where Garfield lives. It's just a few hundred yards away.

Flyball Winners

If you're a flyball enthusiast, you've heard of the village of Caledonia. It's southwest of Hamilton and the home of a border collie named Flash who's the North American flyball champion.

Flyball, by the way, is a sport introduced about 10 years ago. A team of four dogs compete in a relay race, jumping hurdles, catching a ball they release from a spring-loaded box, and carrying it back to the starting line.

Flash is the anchor of the Caledonia team which is called Border Patrol. The famous foursome has competed all across Canada and down through the United States. They were undisputed champions when I first saw them.

It was at a training session held in a farmer's field on the outskirts of the village. The dogs' trainers were there and a few spectators shouted encouragement as each dog took its turn.

Flash, or course, was the star. His speed was amazing. As I recall, the course was about 45 yards long, and I'll swear Flash covered it up and back in six or seven seconds.

One of his teammates was Tyme, who was also the mother of some of his 26 offspring. Tyler was another member of Border Patrol, and a son of Flash. The most lovable of the team was a big shaggy dog named Woody. While the other dogs blazed over the course, Woody shuffled along, getting over the hurdles in an awkward way, while the spectators shouted, "Come on, Woody." He's not used to competition, but he's popular during the warmups, and the other dogs like him. Apparently, he settles them down.

Doug Smuck, who owns and trains Flash, said that invitations to compete south of the border have become fewer and fewer. "It's their game, but we beat them most of the time and I suppose they don't like it," he laughed.

Border Patrol's toughest competition is a team called The Renegades. They're always hot on their heels. And the surprising thing about it is that The Renegades are based in Caledonia! So, I guess that makes Caledonia the Flyball Capital of the Continent.

Getting There

Caledonia is on Highway 6 south of Hamilton. On summer evenings the champs often have a workout in a field just beside the highway as you go into town.

Lily Beck

❦

Lily Beck is a dynamic little woman in her '80s who's an expert in porcelain art. She lives on the outskirts of Port Dover, a village on Lake Erie's north shore, in a large bungalow surrounded by magnificent landscape gardening.

We were there on a beautiful summer morning. The gardens were in full bloom. There were rose bushes, shrubs and flowers on two levels, and below that, a big vegetable garden. And Lily does all the landscaping and gardening herself! It's amazing to think that an elderly woman -- 5'1", weighing about 100 pounds -- could manage to create and maintain such an extensive project. But to Lily, it's "just a hobby," as she puts it. Her real work is painting porcelain and teaching others the ancient art.

Her spacious home is packed with porcelain pieces. There are figures, figurines, and plates everywhere you look. There's a cabinet of porcelain dolls. Even the lace on their clothing is glazed.

Downstairs in a big workshop are more of the painted treasures. A wondrous array that intrigues visitors and students alike. They wander around before classes, admiring the work their teacher has done over the years.

Painting porcelain is a tricky operation. It begins with a design. The paints come in a powder form and are mixed with oil on a palette. Special brushes are used and the most difficult thing for the student is learning the strokes. They have to be done with meticulous care.

When completed, the pieces are fired in a kiln up to 1200 degrees Fahrenheit to give the paint permanence. Overheating can cause disastrous results. I saw one overheated vase that is kept as an example. It looked like the Leaning Tower of Pisa.

"After you start painting, you begin to notice things around you, how they grow and the beauty that surrounds them," Lily explained to the students.

As we were leaving, Lily mentioned she was off to a convention of the Porcelain Art Guild in the States. "I get to three or four seminars a year," she said. "There's always something new to learn."

I glanced back at the tiny lady as she walked quickly down into the vast garden. She was 82 at the time. A ball of fire. Fit as a fiddle. Always on the move. An unforgettable personality.

Getting There

Lily lives at 20 Emily Street. Call first at 519-583-2777 to get exact directions.

Lifestyles of the Rich and Feathered

❦

It's not like too many people around the province have heard of Empire Corners. It's near Cayuga and as far as I could see consists of a few houses and one or two service stations. But it's a familiar name to those interested in exotic birds. That's because Debbie Kinloch's parrot farm is located on the outskirts of the hamlet.

About 175 birds are lodged in an old barn behind the Kinloch farmhouse that borders Highway 56. They greet you with a

cacophony of chatter and shrill noises, but your attention soon turns to their vivid coloring. The old barn is lit up with every colour of the rainbow.

There's a breeding pair of lilac crowned Amazons that caught my eye and a rare Trinton cockatoo. Debbie was hand-feeding a couple of red-bellied parrots. Many of the birds were born and bred right at the farm. There's an incubator room and a nursery where there were about 20 parrot chicks with beaks wide open, waiting to be fed. Believe me, there's never a dull moment in the old barn.

The farm is the culmination of a dream for Debbie. She's been interested in birds and animals since childhood. Born in Florida, she says that when she was a little girl she'd make a map of where bird nests were located in her neighborhood and keep track of the days on which the eggs were hatched. Later, she studied zoology, and her first job was as a dogcatcher in the Rockies of Colorado. When she came to Ontario, she cared for the falcons at North Bay Airport.

Eventually she was able to buy the farm and import a few parrots. That was six years ago and, in that relatively brief period, she's become the well- known breeder of the birds.

I watched Lorraine Marcotte, who helps Debbie, wheeling a food cart around the barn. Each of the adult birds has its own dish. Together, they require at least six pounds of pellets a day, along with fruit and vegetables.

They're a noisy bunch, but it doesn't seem to bother Debbie and Lorraine. They give the birds the V.I.P. treatment -- the finest in food, even personalized manicures. It all adds up to "Lifestyles of the Rich and Feathered."

Getting There

Take Highway 6 west out of Hamilton to Jarvis. Go south on Highway 3. Go through Cayuga to highway 56, which takes you into Empire Corners. Debbie's place is nearby. Ask at the gas stations. Phone 905-772-5639.

Clock Watchers

Strathroy is a tidy town of ten thousand west of London. It has an interesting main street. The Ogilvie flour mill is at the top of it. They mill grains grown by farmers in the surrounding countryside. There are both old and new buildings as you drive down the street, and a variety of shops. Among them is Pogue Jewelers.

From the outside, Pogue's appears to be the usual sort of jewellery business, and blends in with the other attractive storefronts. But people in the know, know that Pogue's is no ordinary jewellery store. It's Strathroy's main tourist attraction. That's because of its clocks. Pogue's has the largest selection of clocks in Ontario, possibly in the whole country.

There are big clocks, miniature clocks, clocks from Europe and Asia. Over 600 of them!

It's not a clock shop, as such. It has a big stock of rings and other jewellery, but as you walk down the aisle past everything else you come upon the clocks. They're everywhere!

There are hand-carved cuckoo clocks from Germany, Italy and China. And for variation, a selection of music boxes, as well as a player piano which enthralls children.

But the most impressive display of all is on the second floor of the store. It's packed with grandfather clocks. At least a hundred of them! They stand there grandly. Dignified. Stately. Their chimes play softly from time to time, giving a feeling of peace and serenity.

Jim Pogue, who started the business 30 years ago, showed me some of his favorites. As we walked down row after row I said, "Jim, I'm sure that tourists like to roam around and look at these expensive beauties, but do many people buy them?"

"You'd be surprised," he replied. "I had one customer who bought one for each of his five children when they got married." He paused, then smiled and added, "At the time I wished he had 10 children."

I spent a few hours at Pogue's but there was still more to see. It takes time to see the whole selection, and the tick-tocks of the hundreds of clocks continue to draw visitors chime after chime.

Getting There

Strathroy is west of London. Take 401 to the Strathroy cutoff. Pogue's is easy to find. It's about halfway down the main street.

Surprise Sarnia

❦

W hen you walk into the Sarnia studio of Keith and Teresa Tovey, you're surrounded by marsh marigolds, jack-in-the-pulpits, trilliums and baskets of autumn leaves.

Their vibrant beauty takes you by surprise. At first glance, they look like the real thing, or possibly made of porcelain. But they're sculpted in leather, of all things!

I've seen leather work before, of course, but mostly belts and purses, or at times leather masks. But this was something different.

I'd made an appointment to see the Toveys. And Keith, a bearded, bespectacled, scholarly-looking young man noticed my quizzical gaze as I gingerly touched the leather leaves and flowers.

"People we see at shows have the same reaction," he smiled. "What we've done is adapt an ancient craft to a portrayal of nature, and to that extent our work may be unique."

Keith's wife, Theresa, was sitting at a workbench using acrylics and dyes to color a Saskatchewan lily, the couple's project at the time.

Teresa put down her brush and looked up. She had a peaches and cream complexion and a braid of brown hair that fell down to her waist. "We hope to do all of the provincial flowers, but it takes time," she said, nodding to the half-finished lily. "Sometimes it takes months to complete a flower."

Keith joined her at the bench, and as I watched them work, I could understand why it was so time-consuming. Even the veins of the leaves had to be hand-tooled.

"The biggest challenge is getting the leather to resemble foliage," said Teresa. "We use techniques that go back to the Middle Ages."

The couple travel extensively to find plants and flowers in their natural habitat. Over in a corner of the studio was a sculpture of a wild orchid. Keith said it was modelled on the orchids that grow in profusion around Tobermory.

The Toveys were preparing for a show at Hamilton's Royal Botanical Gardens when we were there. I took a look at some of the price tags on the sculptures they'd set aside for display at the show. They were in the $2,000 range, which wasn't out of line considering the artistry involved.

Apparently there are about four craftspeople in the province working exclusively in leather, but the Toveys are the only ones doing nature studies. And there's no question they're in a class by themselves. Place their works in any woodlot and they wouldn't look out of place.

Getting There

Take Highway 402 from London to Sarnia. Phone the Toveys at 519-344-5867 and get directions to their home.

Canada's Oldest Private Eye

❦

A couple of years ago, I met my first Private Eye. For some reason I've never had the opportunity to actually meet a bona fide Private Investigator. My experience has been limited to fictional characters like Sam Spade or Mike Hammer.

They always seemed to have cluttered cubby hole offices in the seedy section of some big city, and were mostly raffish-looking types. The one I met didn't fit the mould at all.

Oh, he was rough and tough all right. He'd been around. He'd been a P.I. for 40 years. He'd seen it all. But his lifestyle was totally different from the usual movie or TV personalities you see.

In the first place, he lives in a comfortable home in the village of Southhampton on the shores of Lake Huron, and his office is in his luxuriously furnished den. His name is Douglas Hopkinson. He's a tall, distinguished looking man. On top of that, he's now 73 years of age, which makes him Canada's oldest still-practicing Private Investigator!

He calls his company "Voyageur Investigations" and has 36 agents scattered across the country. All are experienced in various types of investigative work. But these days Doug and his crew are concentrating on what he calls Biological Research Investigations. That involves tracing birth mothers of those who were adopted, finding lost loves or investigating "Mysterious disappearances."

It's time-consuming work. Doug uses computers, a fax machine and is frequently getting phone calls, or making them to faraway places. He says Biological Research is mostly just constant intensive digging.

It wasn't always that way. Scattered around the den are relics of his razzle-dazzle days when he was a gumshoe in the city. There's a periscope, a white cane, bugging equipment and a mannequin he calls "Doris." The mannequin came in handy when he was tailing someone. "A man sitting in a parked car with his girlfriend looks a lot less suspicious than somebody sitting there by himself," he laughs. "In my time, I guess I planted about 500 bugs, but when the Privacy Act came in, they went around collecting listening devices from investigators."

Doug can tell you stories from his long career that would make your hair stand on end. But now he's switched from leg work to head work, as befits Canada's oldest practising Private Eye.

Getting There

The head office of Doug's international operation is at 430 Birch Street in Southhampton (north of Goderich on the road map) Phone 519-797-5177. He knows what he's doing and has an extensive knowledge of investigative and intelligence work, along with a great sense of humour.

Ontario's Best Kept Secret

❦

The world's first oil well wasn't discovered in some exotic faraway land, but in the little village of Oil Springs, southeast of Sarnia. If you were unaware of this intriguing slice of our history, you're not alone. It's Ontario's best-kept secret!

Today, Oil Springs is a quiet community, typical of the many small towns in southwestern Ontario. But in 1858, when James Miller Williams dug down just 14 feet to strike oil, and later when the first gusher blew in with a tremendous roar that ripped over the countryside, Oil Springs became the gaudiest, most delirious boom town North America had ever known!

In those heady years, hundreds of thousands of barrels of oil flooded the fields. The drillers, the muckers and the speculators couldn't believe it. The phenomenon was the wonder of the age!

What happened here in Ontario had to be far more important than what happened in the California and Klondike gold rushes. And the events of the exciting era are faithfully recorded at the Oil Museum of Canada on the outskirts of the village. There are models of early oil rigs, an impressive variety of artifacts, rock formations and photos of the pioneers at work.

The curator, Donna McGuire, has an encyclopedic knowledge of it all, and can tell you hair-raising stories about the riotous days of the winners and the losers, and how the men of Oil Springs and near-by Petrolia later travelled to foreign countries to show the world how to find and bring in oil.

But there's more! The pungent odor of crude still hangs over the village. And near the main street you can see rusty pumps creaking away. They look like giant crickets and, although they may be old and forgotten by many Canadians, they're still pumping oil!

That's right. There are about 400 wells operating. The equipment is ancient, but the wells produce about 26,000 gallons of oil a year.

Many of these wells are owned by the Fairbank family. One of the first oilmen in the district was J.H.Fairbank, and his great-grandson, Charles Fairbank, is still working the fields.

"Young Charlie," as everybody calls him, grew up in the area and in the tradition. Later, he became a high school teacher, but the lure of black gold eventually took over and he left teaching to run the family's properties.

I've met him a couple of times over the years. I remember watching Charlie and a crew adjusting an old jerker rod. It was an original used by his great-grandfather in the early days.

I went over and, in the course of the conversation, asked why he didn't replace the creaking equipment with modern machinery. "There's no need," he smiled. "It's a good method. It works."

He was right. It's living history. And, although the song may have ended, the melody still remains as you sniff the pungent odor that's a reminder of a highlight in our history.

Getting There

Take 401 to 402 just west of London. 402 leads to Sarnia. About 10 miles this side of Sarnia, turn south at Highway 21 through Wyoming, past Petrolia to Oil Springs. The museum is on the outskirts of the village.

Central and Eastern Ontario

Tyrone Mill

🍎

The quiet charm of the country hamlets like Tyrone puts you in a mellow mood. Located just north of Bowmanville, it has a general store, some snug houses, a tiny community centre, and down the road a bit is the Tyrone Mill.

In yesteryear, every community worth its salt had its own mill, and Tyrone was no exception. But today, the mill sets Tyrone apart, since it's one of the few remaining water-powered mills in the province.

It dates back to 1864, and was originally a grist mill. When modern methods of making flour took over, it was converted into a sawmill, and the ancient equipment is still powered by water from the pond beside the mill. The power turns a turbine, the most modern thing in the mill. It's a mere sixty years old.

You can watch logs being rolled onto a carriage which takes them to a big whirling saw and then to a planer which finishes the rough timber. The old machines work with a will turning out custom lumber. And it's fascinating to see the gears, pulleys and belts going round and round, sending power energy to the sawmill.

In more recent years, an old apple cider press was installed in one corner of the building. It operates from September to April, and people from the surrounding area bring in their apples to be turned into cider.

The present owner, Robert Shafer, is a heritage conscious young man who hopes to restore the flour-making process. He's already acquired two massive mill stones and he sharpens them daily in preparation for the time when they'll be in use once again.

Since he took over, Shafer has turned the place into a commercially viable operation despite numerous setbacks. Visitors and

Bill, cameraman Rick Dade, and Eric Chernacki, one of Bill's grandchildren at the old mill. In yesteryear every community worth its salt had a mill. Photo by Linda Chernecki

school children are always coming and going, and when I was there, the sawmill and cider press were going full blast.

It's quite an accomplishment to combine history with a profitable operation. It's been a tough job restoring and maintaining the wonderful old mill. And it's not over yet. But as Shafer says, where there's a mill there's a way.

Getting There

Go north on Liberty Street, Bowmanville's main street. A few miles north you'll run smack into the village of Tyrone. Turn left, go down the hill and you'll see the mill.

The Smallest Jail

The old Creemore jail. It's no ordinary jail. It brings smiles 'n chuckles. It's squat. It's just 20 feet long and 15 feet wide. In the old days, three guests was a full house. Tourists love it. Historians love it. It stands proudly. It should, Creemore people say. It's the smallest jail on the continent!

The little jail blends right in with the village itself. Located where the Mad and the Noisy Rivers meet (their real names), people saunter along the block-long main street, browse around in The Gaggle of Geese and other shops and boutiques, or perhaps jaywalk over to the venerable Sovereign Hotel.

Artists are drawn to the village. One of them is Harold Donnelly. Harold and his wife Grace live across from the jail, which hasn't done any real business in years. Even it its heyday it was usually limited to an occasional inebriate collected for an overnight stay by the lone constable.

The last time it was used officially, it housed an 8-year-old boy, and a man who had quaffed too many. The boy had hitched a ride with the man. Since it was late he stayed overnight, and was returned to his house the next day. The boy is now an 80-year-old who's alive and well and living in Creemore.

By the late '30s, the jail had been abandoned and gradually fell into disrepair. A few years ago, the Donnelly's, who had always been conscious of its historical value, decided it should be preserved. They approached the Lions Club and the Council about the situation and it was agreed the jail should be restored.

Today, it's quite a tourist attraction. The three small cells are furnished the way they were in the old days. Just simple amenities. The Donnelleys are volunteer caretakers and had a couple of caps made

up with ''Warden'' printed on them. Visitors get quite a kick out of
it. The jail is no Bastille, Millhaven or Alcatraz. But it has distinc-
tion. It has a style of its own. After all, it's the smallest little slammer
on the continent.

Getting There

*Go north from Barrie on Highway 27. Take Highway 28 to Stayner. Keep
going west on Stayner's main street to county road 42, then go south to Creemore.*

A Magic Piano

Y ou'd think that the only piano of its kind in the world would be
in some exclusive salon in London, Paris, or perhaps Vienna. But it's
not. It's in the Central Ontario town of Bowmanville.

The piano was built at the turn of the century by the Bowmanville Piano and Organ Company, at that time the second-largest
piano company in the country. An upright with a concert grand action, it was intended as a showpiece for the company. Local artisans
were hired to handcraft statuettes in its magnificent mahogany. The
skill of the firm's top piano craftsmen were utilized to make the
piano unique. It was later sent on a tour of music capitals of Europe,
and won prizes everywhere, including first prize at the 1904 Chicago
World's Fair.

Eventually, the piano was bought by John Jury, a well-known
Bowmanville businessman. But as time went on, it fell into disrepair.
In the early '60s, the Jury family home became the Bowmanville
Museum, and a part-time guide, Tom Webb, thought it was a shame
that such an outstanding piano was just standing there as a prop in
the parlour.

Tom had retired and gone to live in Bowmanville in 1985 and, although he was a newcomer, he though he'd try to raise some money locally to put it back in shape. He made a few enquiries and discovered that restoring the old instrument would cost about $5,000.

He was able to convince Wintario to put up half the cost if he could raise the other half. He began a campaign on a small scale. Then the Bowmanville newspaper published a picture of Tom standing beside the piano and a story about the project. The money started to roll in and within three months the required funds had been raised.

The piano was taken to the workshops of Clarke Pianos in Port Perry, and after considerable work, was completely restored. Finally it was returned to its home at the museum, and Tom began to refer to it as "The Magic Piano". I asked him why.

"There are several reasons," he smiled. "I achieved a certain degree of recognition in the community as a result of heading the drive. Since I was relatively new to the town, I'd been sort of anonymous, but during the drive I met all sorts of people. To me, there was something magical about it. Not only that, when I play or listen to it, there seems to be a special sound. I call it magic," he said.

School children now come to the museum to listen to well-known musicians play "The Magic Piano" as part of their musical appreciation courses. The day I was there, Tom himself was playing, and a small group of children listened attentively.

When he had finished, I went over to compliment him on his efforts to restore the famous old piano. "Just a case of one old crock helping another," he cracked.

Getting There

Take 401 to Bowmanville which is about 8 miles east of Oshawa. Take the Liberty Street exit. That's the main street. Follow it to the centre of town. As I recall, there's a sign directing you to the museum. When you see the piano look for the hand-carved figures on the sides. They're unusual.

The Old Master

Fifty years ago, John Van Huizen was a bookbinding apprentice in Amsterdam. Today, he practices his craft in a little shop on Secord Street in St. Catharines, binding and restoring books the way it was done centuries ago.

People bring in old bibles and antique books that are battered, beaten and broken, and in some way or another John manages to rejuvenate them.

It's not a craft you can learn overnight, and the books aren't restored overnight! It takes hours and hours of delicate, meticulous workmanship that requires exceptional skill and the patience of a saint.

I watched him lift up the frazzled pages of an ancient-looking book. He put acid-free paper behind one of the pages and, with a small tool, carefully straightened the worn sections.

Later, he sewed restored pages of another book on a sewing frame. His hands moved quickly. The pages were sewn together and I could see the binding process developing.

John took me over to a corner of the shop where several vintage tools of the craft were hung on the wall. "You'll notice this sewing frame made back about 1800 isn't too different from the one I'm using now," he said in his Dutch accent.

He showed me how he replaced leather covers. The leather was cut to size, and using appropriate letters from the wide variety of type on hand, he took the type of another machine and pressed the name of the book into gold foil. It looked simple enough, but I wouldn't want to try it.

I also learned something about what's called marbling. It's the process of transforming end covers of a book from a plain cover to

The pages may be frazzled and the old books battered and beaten, but John Van Huizen, the Master bookbinder, brings them back to life.

an intricately-patterned one, which was a popular feature during the Victorian era.

Before leaving, I looked around once more and marvelled at John's craft and his dedication to it. It was apparent that success in the modern age using tradition methods was a way of life in that busy little Old World shop.

Getting There

Take the Queen Elizabeth Way to St. Catharines, and turn off at the Lake Street exit. You'll come to a stop light almost immediately. Turn right and go a couple of blocks to Secord Drive. Turn right and you'll see John's shop a few doors down on the left. It's number 36.

The Perfect Butter Tart

How sweet it is. The perfect butter tart. It's packed with heavenly filling fit for the gods. It's not concocted in some exotic kitchen in faraway places. The perfect butter tart's home is in a tiny bakery in the little village of Brooklin, north of Whitby.

Therein lies a tale. Barb's bakery, a small, attractive shop on Brooklin's main street, began selling butter tarts made by a local lady named Cora Heib. Barb Hulley and her husband John had just taken over the business and soon noticed that customers were grabbing up the tasty tarts and coming back for more.

Then in a timely twist of fate, a food critic for City and Country Home magazine wrote that after a worldwide search he had failed to find the perfect butter tart.

Mail poured in to the magazine. Among the letters were those proclaiming that the perfect butter tart did exist, and could be found in the village of Brooklin.

I heard about all the fuss and, recalling my days as a bushy-tailed, hard-nosed investigative reporter, I traced the source of the phenomenon to Cora Heib's kitchen, a couple of blocks away from the bakery.

The kitchen was the usual type you find in the average bungalow, but there were tarts everywhere. Delicious looking tarts, dozens and dozens of them. Cora, a jolly woman with a ready smile, had predictably been a busy baker since the publicity mills began touting her tarts.

Cameraman Rick Dade set up his lights. Cora wasn't phased a bit. She kept on rolling pastry, cutting it, putting in the delectable filling, and sliding it all off to the oven. She said it took her about six hours to make sixteen dozen tarts.

I asked her the obvious question. "Cora," I said, "What are the ingredients that make your tarts so special?"

I should have known better. She gave me a quizzical glance, rolled her eyes a bit and smiled slightly. Something like the Mona Lisa. Mysteriously. But she uttered nary a word.

Back at Barb's Bakery, people were coming in to snap up the tarts. "We go through up to eighty a week since that article appeared. We've had visitors from all over. We just can't keep up with the demand," enthused Barb.

I sat down at a table at Barb's and had a butter tart. I had controlled myself. It was my first. Cameraman Rick, who has the heart of a ten-year-old rascal, had already sneaked a few in Cora's kitchen.

I savoured the delicacy of the tart while thinking that the secret of this nectar, possibly coveted even by the gods of Olympus, remained, and would likely always remain, with Cora. Pity.

Getting There

Take Highway 12 north from Whitby. It's a short drive to Brooklin. The main street isn't very big. You'll see Barb's Bakery easily. If you have a sweet tooth you're in for a treat.

Ponderosa

❦

The famed orchards and vineyards of the Niagara Peninsula are etched in my childhood memories. Part of my youth was spent in the district, and I guess I snitched more than a few peaches and bunches of grapes from farmer's fields. But in the early '20s the land bore good fruit for miles and miles, so it's unlikely my playmates and myself ate enough to put much of a dent in production.

As I recall, places like Thorold were just little villages at the time. But when I went back last year to do a story I had to wind my way through the traffic of a small city to get to my destination.

It was a 12-acre spread of placid ponds and lush lawns amid channels, inlets, outlets and small windmills. In the ponds were fish. No ordinary fish. They were Japanese Koi, the same hybrid that glide about at the White House and at the Imperial Palace in Tokyo. The Japanese revere the fish which they've raised for 3,000 years. And the Koi are expensive. One fish has been known to sell for $10,000.

The farm is operated by Gary and Sandra Desy. Coincidentally, the land was originally part of a vineyard owned by Gary's parents, and I was thinking I might possibly have sampled some of their grapes in the old days.

We wandered around looking at the fish. They were big, vibrantly colored in orange, white, red, even blue. They can grow up to 40 pounds and some live for 40 years. Their value is determined by their markings. If there's a blurred line between the colors, their worth decreases. The Desys have had Koi that sold as high as $2,000, but most of the ones we saw were about $100.

The Koi need lots of care. Aside from feeding, they must be transferred periodically to medication tanks as a preventative measure. Others have to be taken to breeding tanks. And, of course, many are kept in display tanks to be sold to people who want them for their own ponds. There are tight security measures, but thieves would have to be experts to tell which fish are the valuable ones. The biggest predators are blue heron and gulls.

Another purpose of the farm is to provide crayfish and fathead minnow for ponds. The crayfish keep down debris, and the minnows consume algae.

Gary has become a specialist on ponds. People with pond problems consult him, and there's an impressive file listing those who have used the service and the excellent results they have had.

The Desys have the only registered Koi farm in Ontario. Children love the place, and seniors revel in the colorful beauty of the fish, and the tranquility of it all. More and more ponds are being added, and the residents of the area nicknamed it The Ponderosa.

Getting There

The Koi Fish Farm is at Thorold's south end. We entered on Highway 20. Better check with the Desy family at 905-892-8990.

Detector's Dream

In the past, I've always looked upon people who roam around sweeping the ground with metal detectors in a very casual way -- with a certain amused indulgence. Then I met Fred and Carol McDonald.

The basement of their home in Oshawa is a treasure house of coins, rings, and a variety of artifacts that stun visitors. And the whole cache was uncovered by their metal detectors!

For over 10 years the couple have scoured land, sea, lakes, rivers and streams in their quest for lost or forgotten items.

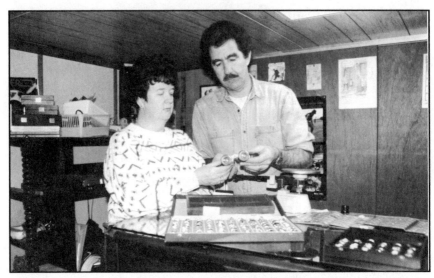

With their metal detectors, Fred and Carol McDonald find all sorts of treasures. They've scoured land and sea looking for loot. Photo by Linda Chernecki.

Since they started, the pair have worked their way up to top-of-the-line detecting equipment and have travelled all over the province and parts of the United States using their highly sensitive detectors in hundreds of parks and beaches. They've become so enthusiastic about the hobby that they've formed a company they call "Detector's Dream" and sell metal detectors and supplies. Fred hopes that when he retires from his job at General Motors he can go into business full time.

The machines sell for three hundred to one thousand dollars, but the McDonalds say they soon pay for themselves. One weekend, Fred and Carol between them found three hundred and twenty-three coins, including 11 loonies, and six rings -- two gold, three silver and one just junk. On Fred's best day, he found 12 rings, most of them while searching underwater. But it's not always that way. At times, all a detector picks up is useless trash.

The McDonalds like to return anything they find to its rightful owner, and often they've been successful.

"People see us in parks or at the beach with our detectors, and come up and ask us if we can find something they have lost," said Carol.

One day at Balsom Lake, a man asked them if they could find his car keys which he'd lost while playing with a frisbee in shallow water. It took Fred 20 minutes to find them. The man jumped up and down in grateful glee.

There are thousands upon thousands of stories in the McDonald's collection. Who knows what heartaches are behind some of those lost loves? But also the joy when the detectives with their detectors uncover some missing treasure for someone. It's all part of the Detector's Dream.

Getting There

Take 401 to Oshawa and go in on the Simcoe Street exit. Go Simcoe north to Adelaide where there's a set of lights. Turn left to Golf Street, then right at Frederick. The detectors live at 115 Frederick. You'll be impressed with the cache they've acquired over the years. The phone number is 905-723-6472.

Junk Art

Syd Abrams and his wife, Joan, live in a luxurious condominium in Toronto's exclusive Forest Hill district. The furnishings are beautiful, but what visitors notice most are the sculptures, the paintings, the vases and other works of art so tastefully displayed. All of them appear to be expensive treasures.

But Syd creates them himself. Not only that, he doesn't use exotic materials, he makes them from trash -- junk! Syd hesitates to use such terms. He prefers to describe the materials he uses as "household discards," although he says it with a twinkle in his eye and a sly grin.

The "household discards" include bleach jugs, styrofoam cups, tins, paper plates, plastic straws or occasionally variations such as slag from foundries. He converts these discards into unusual and highly attractive abstract sculptures, most of them finished with gold coloured spray.

The idea was born one morning a couple of years ago when the Abram's children and grandchildren joined them for a family breakfast. Just as Joan was going to clear away the disposables cluttering the kitchen counter, Syd said, "Wait! Don't throw those out! I have an idea!"

He picked up a plastic orange juice bottle, heated it over the stove and with a few deft twists, forged a human figure. Then using a piece of leftover ceramic tile as a base, he assembled a cast-off bowling ball and pin belonging to his granddaughter with some bits of rigatoni with the figure to create his first sculpture. He dug out some spray paint and lacquer and ended up with a remarkable piece that had the apparent solidity of bronze.

Of course that wasn't his only foray into the arts. Even during the years when active Abrams, now 78, was operating the steel company which he sold some years ago, he was enjoying his hobby of painting.

However, once he started with his new kind of sculpture, he became obsessed. He's molded well over 100 pieces. There are sailing ships, whimsical animals and people. His imagination is unbridled.

Syd has had a one-man show at a Toronto gallery and he hopes to have his pieces displayed someday at New York's Museum of Modern Art. And why not? As Syd said, "I like to think of it as 21st century hi-tech sculpture."

Getting There

Syd and Joan live on Toronto's Heath Street. Phone first. I've never seen anything quite like Syd's stuff. It's amazing what he's done with junk.

Field of Dreams

❦

I was having a coffee at the general store in the hamlet of Brentwood while waiting for cameraman Rick Dade. I knew he couldn't miss me because downtown Brentwood consists of the general store, a church, and a few houses. Until recent years not too many people were likely aware that the hamlet even existed. That all changed when word got around about Wally Dickenson's Field of Dreams and Market Garden.

When Rick arrived we drove a couple of hundred yards to the outskirts of Brentwood where Wally's place is located. It's not a big set-up, but there are a hundred and fifty varieties of vegetables, and unless you know something about gardening, you can become bogged down in utter confusion.

Take tomatoes, for example. There are purple, banana, acid-free and yellow varieties. Then there are peppers in black, brown, blue, orange, red, yellow and green. Add to that tobacco, twelve-foot high corn, and cotton, of all things!

In the background is a miniature village, and carved out in the corn patch a small Field of Dreams, as in the movie of the same name. That's the one where the ghosts of Hall of Fame baseball players came back to play after the hero heard a voice telling him to build a ball field in the middle of his corn.

Wally was saying good-bye to some visitors as we pulled into the driveway. He walked over to greet us. Well, he didn't exactly walk. Wally never walks. He sort of darts from place to place. And he talks fast. A machine gun kind of delivery. Like his veggies, he's not your average home-grown type. He's rather short, thin but wiry, bespectacled, and in his straw hat and overalls reminded me of a barnyard elf of some kind.

"Come and see my village," he enthused, leading us over to a little church, a schoolhouse, a barn and other buildings.

"Most of the things here I knew when I was a child in Singhampton. I took a course in drafting and made them to scale - one inch to a foot."

Rick and I were impressed. Noticing our glances of admiration, Wally smiled with glee, skipped around to the side of the little church and opened up the roof. There was a tiny organist playing hymns. The recorded music began as the roof was lifted.

Wally made everything down in his basement workshop from recycled materials. Even his tools are off-beat. His saw was ingeniously constructed from an old sewing machine.

But his favorite is his Field of Dreams. A small baseball diamond beside his crop of corn. There are bleachers and he's hooked up lights with minuscule bulbs.

A self-admitted dreamer, Wally's projects are a combination of history and fantasy. People are coming all the time to enjoy his creations. So far no famous ball players from the past have appeared. But who knows? With dreamers anything can happen.

Getting There

Take Highway 27 north from Barrie to Highway 28. Go west to Sunnidale Corners, then south on County Road 10. Brentwood is a few miles down the road. Everybody knows Wally's place. Ask at the general store.

Barn Raising

Every time we drive through the Markham or Stouffville districts, my mind drifts back to a barn raising some years ago in the nearby village of Vandorf. It was the first step in the recreation of a complete family farm at the Whitchurch-Stouffville Museum and was the first community-style barn raising there in 25 years. But it was nothing new to some of the farmers who were involved.

The barn, originally built about 1850, was donated to the museum. It had been carted in pieces from a farm a few miles from Vandorf.

About 30 men worked on the job. None of them were using nails. The parts were pinned together with wooden pegs. One of the older men watching the others was saying that's why old barns lasted so long. They weren't as rigid and gave way with the wind.

Before the raising began, the workers were given a typical farm meal. Morley Symes was one of the crew. In his day he had built more than 300 barns. Everybody was asking him questions. I guess he was sort of an advisor.

Jim Rae was there. He'd raised a lot of barns too, and was the work captain on the job. He was telling the others that it would likely be the last barn raising in the area.

Finally, everything was ready. We went back out to the barn and people began to gather around it. Jim Rae started to call out "Heave -- Push." The pike poles were on one side, the ropes on the other. Some of the spectators joined the workers. Slowly, the side of the barn went up.

I got the feeling I was watching something I might never see again, as Jim had said. Standing beside me was a wide-eyed boy, about seven years old. I visualized him in years to come telling his grandchildren that away back in the 1980s he once saw an old-fashioned barn raising in a little hamlet called Vandorf.

Getting There

You can see the barn among the many other old buildings in a wonderful outdoor heritage village at the museum in Markham. The museum is located at the northern end of the main street. The guides will show you around.

Cookstown Greens

For years now, one of the old refrains hammered home by moms has been "Eat your greens, they're good for ya."

When I was a kid I didn't like spinach. I didn't know any other kids that liked spinach. I doubted that there was anybody in the whole world who liked spinach. I didn't like lettuce much either. I only ate the stuff because my mom said, "No greens, no dessert." That did it. End of discussion.

But these days, with nutritious lifestyles all the rage, greens are standard fare in gourmet restaurants. But chefs in these upscale places, however, started to complain that they couldn't get the high-quality ingredients they wanted for their salads.

Chef David Cohlmeyer, owner of the Beggar's Banquet in Toronto, was one of them. He decided to do something about it. He sold his restaurant and opened a greenhouse complex near the village of Cookstown to grow vegetables, herbs and flowers -- organically.

We visited Cookstown Greens, as it's called, one morning in early spring. The trees were just beginning to bud. It was a bit nippy that morning, but when we went inside the greenhouse, the air smelled of summer -- damp earth and herbs. There was everything from brilliant shizanthus flowers to buckwheat seedlings and oak-leaf lettuce. There were rolling tables heaped with earth and crowned with masses of herbs. There was a spreading Scotia filbert geranium that had been carried from British Columbia.

Several people were working around the complex. Some were caring for the gardens, others preparing ingredients for the salads. What was most surprising, however, was that the salads were being made on the spot by Cohlmeyer himself!

I watched as he washed and dried various herbs and flowers, mixed them up and put the completed salads into zipbags. The bags were to be delivered to his customers in Toronto.

As I left, clutching a bag of mixed herbs and flowers, I was thinking that moms everywhere would be pleased with Cookstown Greens salads. They're about as green as you can get.

Getting There

Take Highway 27 north to the village of Thorton which is a few miles south of Barrie. Go west on Robert Street to Concession 9. Turn left and go south about a mile and you'll see the greenhouse on the right hand side of the road.

Willie may look tough, but he's as gentle as the family dog, and a big hit with children who visit the farm. Photo by Kevin Smith.

Willie the Bull

Willie the bull leaned his head over the top rail of the fence and gave me a nudge on the shoulder. I was trying to take notes at the time and didn't pay much attention to him.

Ordinarily, I'd make a very fast exit if a strange bull weighing close to a ton was starting to push me around. But I'd met Willie earlier in the day and fed him a couple of carrots. I figured that made us good buddies.

Actually, Willie, Zilo, Kilo and Bera have a lot of buddies. The four are shaggy Highland cattle and a great attraction at Elbrook Farm on the outskirts of the village of Edgar, south of Orillia.

The farm is owned by Peter and Marilyn Marchildon. They have big Belgian horses and other livestock, and schoolchildren go there to get a taste of farm life. They go for a sleigh or hay ride in the woods, skate on one of the brooks in the winter, and toast marshmallows and whatnot over an open fire. It's a change of pace for city kids and a learning experience for them.

But the Highland cattle are the big attraction for the youngsters and other visitors as well. With their long, shaggy, light-brown coats and huge horns, they remind you a bit of prehistoric mammoths. They look tough, and they can get nasty if wolves or coyotes come sneaking around. But they're as gentle and friendly with visitors as the farm's big jovial dog.

Marilyn carries a bag of carrots so people can give them a snack. All you have to do is hold out a carrot and whistle, and they'll come trotting over. They reach out and eagerly gobble up the goodies.

They're an ancient breed that originated in the Highlands and west coastal islands of Scotland. I found it interesting that Highland cattle raised in Canada are gaining quite a reputation for quality. And Marilyn said that even Scottish breeders are now buying Canadian cattle to improve their own herds.

Getting There

Take Highway 400 extension north of Barrie to Highway 93. Go north on 93 to the hamlet of Dalston. You'll see a general store. Turn right (east). Go through the village of Edgar and in a few hundred yards you'll see a small sign saying "Elbrook Farms." I missed the sign the first time around and had to go back to Edgar to get directions.

The Old Sport Co.

The village of Creemore proudly bills itself as "100 years behind the times." It's true that most of the buildings on the main street are at least a century old. Most have been restored and converted into shops and boutiques.

The village is nestled in a valley south of Collingwood where "The Mad" and "The Noisy" rivers converge, and you find shops like "The Mad River Bakery" and so forth. Among these old-timers is "The Old Sports Company," which is known coast to coast by sports memorabilia collectors. It's located in a former gas station of the '20s, which was turned into an antique shop and now is chock-full of old sports items. They seem to reach out and touch your memories of other eras.

The old place houses a truly amazing cornucopia of sport stuff of yesteryear, guaranteed to astound even the most jaded of veteran fans and collectors. It's likely the largest collection of its kind in the country.

There are old football helmets of the kind worn by Canada's greats like Conacher, Ted Reeve, Harry Batstone and Norm Perry. (As kids, we called this game "Rugby") There are vintage skates, about 40 different kinds, including spring skates. There's a pair of 1891 roller skates and an indoor baseball as big as a bowling ball. There are golf clubs galore, dating back to the days of Bobby Jones. The good old sport behind all this is big John Simpson, an imposing six-footer-plus who left his nine-to-five job because, as he puts it, he "inherited an acquiring mind." His parents were antique collectors and he became interested in collecting sports-related items as a child.

John travels extensively to get additional things for his already-bulging establishment. He finds a lot of it at estate sales, and, since he's well-known as an appraiser, if people bring in things to see if they're worth anything he might buy the item from them right on the spot. If it's in disrepair, he'll get it back into condition in his workshop at the back of the store.

The assortment seems endless -- from yesteryear's posters to Ty Cobb baseball bats, sleds, and bric-a-brack you wouldn't believe.

Sports fans and collectors are coming and going all the time. They browse and buy, and the older ones leave with a faraway look in their eyes.

Getting There

See directions for "The Smallest Jail" (p. 118) to get to Creemore. The Old Sport Company is on the main street. Look for an ancient looking former service station on the left hand side of the street. That's it.

A Curious Business Venture

The Creator must have chuckled when making ostriches. They can't soar like an eagle, haven't the grace of the gull, nor the beauty of the swan. They're ungainly birds, with their long necks, middle-age spread and spindly legs.

But they don't seem to mind. They're a curious, gregarious, fun-loving lot, and valuable for their feathers, meat and hides. Some are eight or nine feet tall and can weigh up to 350 pounds. They're vegetarians and are easy to raise. But if you intend to raise them, be sure to have some ready cash. A mating pair can cost a cool $45,000!

I learned all of this from Eric Bennett, who has an ostrich farm on the outskirts of the village of Campbellford, east of Peterborough. I was unaware that ostrich ranches even existed in Ontario, but Eric said there were at least 20 of them around the province.

As he showed me around, he was telling me he had sold his furniture business in Campbellford to finance the venture. One reason was he wanted to go into farming in some sort of way. He checked around and thought there might be a good market for ostriches, which are considered a delicacy by some people.

"Right now," he said, "I can see it as profitable just to breed them. But over a period of five to 10 years, the supply will be greater, prices will drop and eventually there will a swing toward their meat, which tastes a bit like beef, although milder."

About a week before my visit, Eric had added a number of emus to the flock. They're slightly smaller than ostriches and not as expensive. For example, you can buy a mating pair for a paltry $15,000!

One mating pair I saw were in a separate pen, and like all mating emus, they fought when they first met. The hen had bit her mate on the neck and a blue ointment had been plastered all over the cut.

An ostrich will lay about 50 eggs a year, but only about half will live. Emus won't lay as many, but the survival rate is better.

We wandered back to the ostrich pens, and a few of the birds trotted over to us. One took a peck at Eric's peaked cap and pulled it off, tossed it away, then ran off. I got the feeling he was laughing.

Before I left, Eric gave me a fact sheet about ostriches. One item said that the big birds can run as fast as 45 miles an hour—faster than any other bird. They can also live up to 80 years of age, and can breed until they're 40 or so. Finally, contrary to popular opinion, ostriches never, never bury their head in the sand.

Getting There

Take 401 east to Highway 30, which is in the Brighton area. Go north to Campbellford. The Bennett family is still involved in the furniture business. Drop into the store and they'll direct you. The biggest ostrich farm in the province is located on Highway 12 just north of Whitby. You can see the birds from the highway.

Have Camels, Will Travel

❦

W hen I think of the village of Binbrook, I think of camels. Not that the tiny community is on the Sahara or anything like that. It's west of Hamilton. But it's where I met Harold Johnston and his camels. To the best of his knowledge, Harold is the only private individual in the province who raises the friendly animals.

It all began as a hobby about 10 years ago. His daughter had been visiting Australia and saw a couple of farms where camels were thriving. When she told Harold about it he began reading everything he could find about the famed beasts of burden.

He discovered that they once inhabited North America, and about 600,000 years ago migrated to Asia, and eventually, Africa. He made further inquiries at a few zoos and finally imported a pair, and housed them in a rented barn on the outskirts of Binbrook. Later, he added two more to the group.

Johnston, a retired businessman, began to think of ways to defray the cost of keeping the camels. Billing himself as "The Camel Baron," he got the word around that he'd be available for shows and events to give camel rides. Before you could say Lawrence of Arabia, he was booked for a variety of affairs in many parts of Ontario, and was over the financial hump.

Harold introduced me to his gangly crew. There was Naomie, her mate Benjamin, Tommy and Charlie. All were dromedaries (one-humped). Camels may be beasts of burden to some, but Harold's camels are pampered pets. They nuzzle up to him and obviously regard him as a real buddy.

Some children from a nearby school came over to see if they could get a ride. Harold hoisted them up on Tommy and Charlie, and the friendly pair walked around in a circle. The kids squealed with

delight. Apparently they thought riding a camel was the greatest thing since dirty hands.

Harold said that when he told people he was going to raise camels, they thought he'd gone bonkers. "My friends in the Rotary Club in Hamilton laughed their heads off. But they stopped laughing when they heard I was getting a hundred bucks an hour at shows," he chuckled.

Harold keeps the camels in Wiarton during the summer months. He hitches an open-air trailer to his panel truck and carts them around. Motorists do a double take when they see the caravan on the highways. And it seems Harold is always on the move, Have Camels -- Will Travel.

All I can tell you is to keep your eye open for Harold around the Wiarton area in the good old summer time.

The Little Rebel

🌾

In 19th century Upper Canada, people would get much of their news at the general store. Not just gossip, but the latest in current events, and various tidbits ranging from porkers to politics.

The general store in the village of Queenston in the Niagara district was owned and operated by a fiery Scot named William Lyon MacKenzie. He'd rant and rave to his customers about the injustices and grasping monopolies of what he called "The Family Compact," the ruling political clan of the day.

MacKenzie wasn't the sort to sit around and twiddle his thumbs about such things. "The Little Rebel," as he became known in later years, bought a press, turned the back room of his store into a print shop and began publishing "The Colonial Advocate," a weekly paper in which he took searing shots at The Family Compact.

In 1825 he moved the paper to Toronto, and his editorial wrath eventually sparked the ill-fated rebellion of 1837.

The building in Queenston which housed the original printing plant was restored in the early '30s, and last year a group of veteran newsman turned what MacKenzie referred to as "the cradle of Canadian journalism" into a printing museum.

I went to see it on a beautiful Indian summer day. I drove through the lush countryside of the Niagara Peninsula past the many orchards and vineyards, and over to historic Queenston. Nestled in the shadow of Brock's monument was MacKenzie House, a squat stone building of old world charm.

The trip brought back many memories. Part of my early childhood was spent in the Niagara district, and one of the former newsmen who helped start the museum was Lou Cahil, a playmate of mine when we were children.

The museum itself took me back to my early newspaper days. There are presses scattered around that I'd forgotten existed. The evolution of printing is portrayed from ancient Japanese woodblock type to a Ludlow machine of the 1910 era which turned out ''hot metal'' -- solid lines of type. That was the standard type of printing until offset took over a few decades ago.

To make the display more realistic, there are veteran printers demonstrating the use of the vintage machines. One of them, William Poole, was setting type by hand. My old friend Lou was telling me the real satisfaction comes from seeing the interest school children take in the process. Poole nodded his agreement. ''So do their parents and grandparents,'' he smiled.

The whole project is a living history lesson, and to those of us who remember the fascinating craft of printing as it existed in yesteryear, it's a real homecoming.

Getting There

Take the Queen Elizabeth way to the Niagara River Parkway exit. That's just before the Queenston-Lewiston Bridge to the U.S.A. Turn left on the Niagara Parkway, then right at the next stop sign and down the encampment to Queenston. Turn right at York Street to MacKenzie Heritage Printing (the official name.) For information as to hours phone 905-682-7203.

Barrie Clipper

Doris Pratt of Barrie is the only person I've ever met who reads a daily newspaper with a pair of scissors in her hand.

She clips items ranging from national and international news to interesting little tidbits, and puts them in a scrapbook. She's been doing it for well over 50 years and when I last saw her she had 16 scrapbooks packed with news!

She had clippings from the tumultuous days of the '30s when Edward VIII abdicated to marry Mrs. Simpson, a divorcee. There are stories of the unemployed riding the rails in search of work during the Great Depression. There's a story about a record snowfall in Winnipeg in 1938 and, on a happier note, the hiring of Barrie's first female police officer in 1936. And in a later story, her marriage to a police sergeant.

Doris, who's now in her late '60s, is no stranger to news. She was a rural correspondent for the Barrie Examiner for 40 years when she lived in the nearby St. Paul district. The paper printed a two-column story about her when she retired from the job.

"I don't have any particular system," said Doris. "I just choose the news that appeals to me personally. I'm interested in some world events, but I get a bigger kick out of the lighter side."

Nevertheless, she has a complete scrapbook about World War II days, both overseas and on the homefront. And there's another complete book on the Kennedy era.

But it's the tidbits that grab your attention. The one I found most appealing was about the smallest plebiscite in Ontario's history.

The story goes back to when Molson's Brewery bought the property just south of Barrie on Highway 400. The area was dry at the time and Molson's wanted a retail outlet. It was legal to make beer, but not to sell it.

The only way around the problem was to hold a plebiscite. But there were only two people involved -- the farmer and his wife who wanted to sell their farm to Molson's. Needless to say, they voted wet, and received a very satisfactory sum for their farm.

You don't find too many things like that in the average history book. But Doris Pratt, the Barrie Clipper, has them.

Getting There

If you're interested in the scrapbooks, give Doris a call. She's listed in the Barrie phone book, or directory assistance will give it to you.

Flower Sculpture

The rooms of the home are filled with flowers. You're surrounded by them. There are orchids, daffodils, African violets, even trilliums. But there's no fragrance, and it's not until you reach out to touch them that you realize they're not real. They're carved from wood!

The carver is Ron Tee, who with his wife Inez lives by the river that cuts through the historic Loyalist town of Napanee, near Kingston.

The flowers brings smiles of delight and admiration from those who see them. I felt a bit silly when I instinctively went up to sniff one, but Ron assured me I was not alone. "Everybody does," he laughed.

To the best of his knowledge, Ron is the only one anywhere to carve flowers out of wood. "I was lucky," he said. "When I retired I wanted to learn carving but I couldn't find a teacher. It was the best thing that could have happened to me, since I likely would have

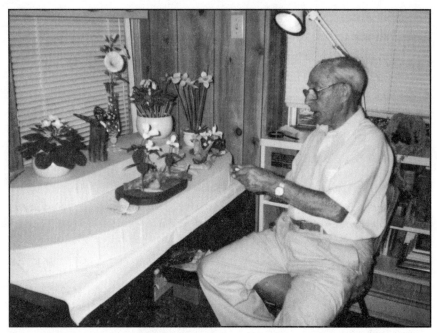

It may take Ron a week to carve a single flower out of wood. Some of his work is spectacular.

ended up carving just the usual things. As it was, I went at it with an open mind.''

He decided to get some books about the craft, and his early attempts resulted, as he puts it, in ''two cut fingers and a big pile of woodchips.''

Finally, he tried carving a swan, and then an orchid, using a piece of his wife's porcelain as a model. This led to other plants and flowers.

Ron took us down to his basement workshop and showed us the tiny tools he uses. He has real flowers as models whenever possible, and it can take him up to 120 hours to carve a single flower, usually from a single block of wood.

He's invented a simple but ingenious cabinet which keeps dust from spreading. Similar to a hospital incubator, it has holes in one side to allow him to slip in his hands and small tools. There's a clear glass lid so he can see what he's working on. The sawdust stays right in the cabinet.

In recent years, he's added butterflies as subjects to carve, and they're nothing short of spectacular. He has one piece showing two butterflies on a piece of driftwood that's particularly appealing.

Ron has won several prizes for the work, and sells some of the items. But he doesn't push it. "I love the craft," he says. "I'm totally wrapped up in it, and that's the only reward I need."

Getting There

Napanee is about 20 miles west of Kingston. Take 401 to the Napanee exit. You'll be on Centre Street. Go south to the four corners at Dundee Street. Ron lives about 5 minutes away from there but it's tricky explaining it. Give him a phone call from there. There's a pay phone at the grocery store near the corner. The number is in the phone book.

Jack's Train

🍎

Jack Brackenburg of Flesherton, south of Owen Sound, is 89 years old, but I'm sure he still has the heart of a 10-year-old boy.

Theoretically, he's "retired," but in the last five years he has probably packed more hours into a pet project than he ever did in a similar period of time during his regular working life.

It all started five years ago when one of his daughters asked him what he'd like for Christmas. Jack said he'd like a little electric train. His daughter got a train, along with a few cars, and gave him the set on Christmas morning.

Jack was very happy with it and after watching it go round and round for awhile, his creative mind and his imagination went into action. He visualized the train running through a village -- places in it named after members of his family. He went down to his basement workshop and built a model train station with a little sign on it signifying the name of the village. The sign read "McGreggor," the middle name of his great-grandson. He built a church and a schoolhouse like the one where Jack went to school in 1913. He added a golf course named after one of his daughters, and a playground for another daughter's children.

He bought more track, and the train began to ramble. Jack decided to build up another area on the railroad line. It became what he called "Canadian". It had a "Peggy's Cove" and a grain elevator. After that Jack threw in things willy-nilly, such as a jungle with a serpent's lair, and a rocket which doubles as a train whistle. Jack is also space minded, and his imagination ran wild on that one. Along with a couple of flying saucers, he put in a space garden. Oh yes, the train also runs by an English castle and a soccer field. But his piece de resistance is his "climbing train." It's 125 feet of track that rises 3/4 of an inch for every foot.

As Jack's project spread out, his bungalow couldn't accommodate it, so he was invited to move it over to the South Grey Museum, which is just across the road from his place. People take pictures of it and marvel at the builder's ingenuity.

When I saw him last, he was working on further additions, and although he's 89 years of age, I'll bet Jack is still one of the busiest men in the village of Flesherton.

Getting There

Jack lives right across from the museum which is on Flesherton's main street. I haven't seen Jack for a couple of years. Check at the museum.

Decoy Champs

As soon as I walked in I found myself in a fowl mood. And I liked it.

I was surrounded by magnificent waterfowl carvings. They filled the shelves lining the recroom walls in the Shanty Bay home of Ian and Joanne Crokam.

The Crokams are waterfowl carvers. Not your average variety. It's a full-time occupation. On top of that, they're world champs!

They have over 300 ribbons they've won at shows all over the continent. Their birds are in a class by themselves.

They showed me a Canvasback Hen decoy, painted in oils. It was judged best in the world in 1992 at the California Open. And a Merganser working bird, judged best in the world at Ocean City, Maryland in 1993. A Ross Goose and a Brant Goose, both world's best. The list went on and on.

They're carved by Ian and painted by Joanne. It takes about four hours to make a simple working decoy, and 300 hours to complete one of the elaborate decorative birds.

Behind the house is a garage with a sign on it reading "The Call of the Loon." It's their trade name, and the garage is Ian's workshop. He carves, sands and drills in the bird's feathers to get them ready for painting.

If he has large orders, such as those from Ducks Unlimited, he turns out duplicates on a vintage machine from the early 1900s, formerly used to make furniture legs.

"The corporate orders like those from Japan and the Ruffed Grouse Society are our bread and butter," said Ian. "Our decorative birds sell for as much as $4,000, but we don't make many of them.

Besides, the service decoys are our biggest interest, the ones that can actually be used.''

We went back into the house when Joanne was doing some intricate painting. Every stroke involved fine detail. As she worked, she mentioned that decoy carving is the only true North American art form that has no European influence.

The Crokams are thought to be the only team of service bird carvers anywhere. They've been making a living at it for over 10 years. They're regarded as the best in the business. And that's nothing to grouse about!

Getting There

The Crokams' place is off Oro Con 3 as you go north on Highway 11 north of Barrie. Give them a call first. It's a bit tricky getting there but not far off the highway. They'll give you exact directions depending on where you are. Phone 705-722-4527.

Vintage Phonographs

The strains of "Yes We Have No Bananas" coming from an old Edison phonograph took me back to my childhood days in the early twenties. From another machine came the strain "It Ain't Gonna Rain No More," another big hit of the era.

The sound was a far cry from Hi-Fi. It was shallow and scratchy. The old tunes had been recorded on "cylinders," Thomas Edison's early experimental records. The phonograph was one of a massive array of vintage machines thought to be the largest in the country. There were over three hundred and fifty of them.

The huge collection was housed in a large climate-controlled stone building in a forested setting near the Unionville home of construction man and developer Dominic de Bernardo. He'd been collecting the ancient machines and associated paraphernalia for about twenty years.

When you first enter the building and see the hundreds of artifacts arranged on shelves that rise up to the high ceiling, you're filled with a sense of wonder.

Veteran cameraman, Rick Dade, who's seen just about every sort of situation during his lengthy career, gazed at the panorama with

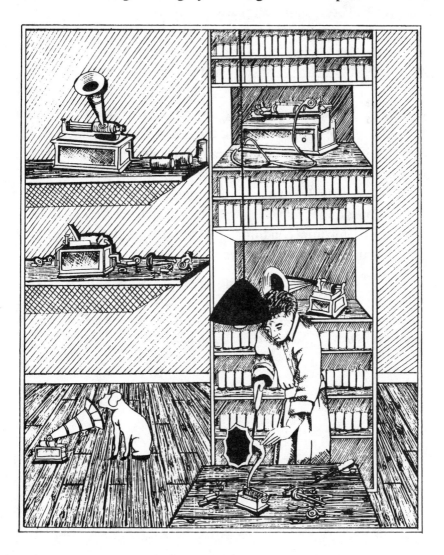

wide-eyed amazement. He gave a low whistle, shook his head slowly, and then began setting up his equipment.

There was plenty to see. There was a bank of twelve thousand cylinders. There were phonographs concealed in lamps. There was another hidden in a small grand piano. There were also several five-foot high brass horns. Dominic explained that they were used to amplify sound in concert halls in the early days. Most of the machines had been built in the early part of the century.

Do you remember "Little nipper", R.C.A. Victor's trade mark? He was the fox terrier whose ear was cocked to hear "his masters voice." The oldest one on display had been made in 1903.

Dominic has restored most of the machines in his basement workshop. He looks upon them as more than just a collection. "When you stop to think about it, they're of historical interest," he said. "I have a feeling future generations might be interested in these old-timers."

He looked fondly at a battered phonograph he had picked up a week before at a flea market. It was obvious that before long it would transformed into mint condition, to join the others in this magnificent display of the wonders of yesteryear.

Getting There

Dominic's home is on 19th Street in Unionville. He's a busy man, but you might be able to catch him at home in the evenings. Be sure to phone first. Ask for directory assistance. It's truly an amazing collection.

The Right Stuff

❧

Harold Boker blew his top when he counted it all up and found he had blown a bundle on chemical fertilizers. He'd been farming in a conventional way for over 30 years. He was fed up with the costs. He bit the bullet. Quit cold turkey and went into organic farming.

Today he has the largest organic farm in Simcoe County. On his 300 acre spread a few miles north of Elmvale, the only fertilizer used is composted manure from his livestock. And what livestock!

He has a herd of Beefalo. They're a cross between full-blooded buffalo and domestic cattle, and are quite at home roaming around Harold's rotated pastures. They're of various shades and colors and have 80% less fat than the usual beef breeds. They feed on plants that domestic breeds leave untouched, and thrive on hay and other roughage.

Then there are the Red Wattle hogs. They don't look like ordinary hogs. They're reddish brown, lean and lively. They live outside all year long in wooden hutches. The sows even have their pigs in small hutches, so the piglets are outside right from birth. Wattle hogs live on grain screens and grain not used for human consumption, and consequently don't compete in the human food chain.

But the mainstay of the farm is the grain. Notably a grain called dinkle or spelt. It's a natural grain, not a hybrid. In the Old Testament, dinkle was praised as the primary bread grain and has been grown since 2500 B.C. in the Rhineland. It's a natural grain and very nutritious. The kernel is enclosed in a strong, hard hull and special milling is required.

To overcome the problem, Harold and his son, Bill, built a state-of-the-art mill in one of the barns. It's four floors of top-flight equipment. They dehull, clean and bag the grain and send it to select dealers and restaurants.

Harold's wife Anne has a small bakery behind the farmhouse, and bakes delicious wholesome bread from dinkle.

Harold is well known by city chefs for his work in the organic field. But perhaps more important, he's always available to share his extensive knowledge with other farmers, and has become known as Simcoe County's Father of Organic Farming.

Getting There

Take Highway 27 north to Elmvale, north of Barrie. Keep going north from Elmvale on 27 about 2 miles. You'll come to a long, gradual hill. The farm is at the bottom of the hill, on the left. Look for the sign.

Stamp of Approval

❦

There are hundreds of working artists in the province, but none whose paintings are like David Outram's works. There are likely only a few artists anywhere whose paintings are similar.

I first saw one of David's paintings at Vance Auctions, a mail order house for stamps run by Vance Carmichael down in the Niagara Peninsula village of Streetsville.

It was a painting of a bluejay standing as a weathercock atop the CN tower. The whole of downtown Toronto could be seen in the lower part of the painting. A birds-eye view, as it were.

I saw it at a distance at first. It seemed to have a strange texture. I walked over to take a closer look and found it wasn't in oils, watercolors or anything like that. It was a collage of stamps.

It took me by surprise. Vance laughed. "People always do a double- take when they see it," he said. "The artist gets a lot of his stamps in bulk from us."

Vance told me the creator of the unusual art form lived in Brockville, and a few weeks later when I was in Eastern Ontario I gave him a call and went to see him at his studio on the outskirts of the city.

Outram, a retired teacher, was a personable, articulate man in his sixties who bubbled with enthusiasm. He told me he had combined his lifelong interest in collecting stamps and painting to begin a new career -- something he calls "stamp art."

Prints of his works are everywhere. Many had to do with nature. At the time, he was working on a "painting" of an owl. Stamps of various countries were being placed over a watercolor he had done first.

"You have to do a regular painting to give you an idea of composition and colour. If you don't do that, you bog down," he said.

Because colour is a main consideration, Outram has a stamp palette on the wall beside his work table. Like a painter's palette, it shows the colours available to the artist. The difference is it has rows and rows of stamps instead of paints.

But doing the painting is only the first step. It's a long process selecting and placing the stamps. It takes about 600 hours to complete a work. The "Toronto Blue Jay," as he calls it, took a full year.

His favorite piece features a Canada Goose and a tough-looking Bald Eagle standing side by side. He calls it "Bonnie and Clyde" and sold the original to a Texas tycoon.

Outram says each of his works requires an average of 450 stamps. Many of the stamps are appropriate for the subject matter.

After he does the original, a maximum of 500 prints are made. If he's particularly pleased with a work, he puts a special stamp in the lower right- hand corner. Obviously, his stamp of approval. He sells the prints at shows and galleries and causes quite a stir among spectators. Unquestionably, artist Outram's off-beat artistry is stamped for success.

David travels a lot and the best way to locate him is to phone Vance Auctions in Streetsville. He's in touch with them frequently to get his stamps.

House of Dolls

❦

The village of Maple Leaf is about 20 miles east of Bancroft. It has a general store, a very attractive restaurant, and a population of about 150. But if you add the inhabitants of the House of Dolls, the population soars by a couple of thousand.

The dolls live in a small cottage you can see from the highway. There are big dolls, little dolls, dolls in all nooks and crannies -- a variety you wouldn't believe.

And that's only the beginning. Outside there's a trail wandering through a forested area called "Memory Lane." You could call it a fairy tale trail. The first thing you see is a life-size Little Red Riding Hood on her way to see her grandmother and that rascal of a wolf. As you walk down the trail, lined with plants and flowers, you pass Alice in Wonderland, and Snow White, Little Boy Blue, sleeping on the job, and poor old Gulliver, fit to be tied.

Leading you down Memory Land is Pearl Crawford, the sole creator of this fantasy land. It's taken her over 30 years to put it all together. Pearl is a petite, active lady who gives visiting children a running commentary about the characters along the trail, and answers the endless questions from their smiling parents.

Pearl has collected the dolls from all sorts of places. But the amazing thing is she's made every stitch of clothing for the two thousand odd dolls!

I asked if she had been a seamstress. "I can't even work with a pattern," she laughed. "When I get a doll, the idea of what it should

be wearing suddenly occurs to me. I guess all of us have a gift of some sort, and that seems to be mine.''

Because of the elements, the dolls out on the trail can't be left out overnight. So Pearl has to bring them in every evening and puts them out again the next morning. That takes about two hours.

After meandering down Memory Lane for a while, I went back to the cottage to take another look at the dolls. Pearl has one doll that's a hundred years old, but she also has what she calls the "commercial" variety. They're movie stars like Cher and Elizabeth Taylor.

Hanging on one of the walls are numerous ribbons the dolls have won, including first prize at the C.N.E. on three occasions.

As I looked around I wondered how many of the lovable dolls could have once belonged to some child. Whatever the case, they've all found a very good home at Pearl Crawford's House of Dolls.

Getting There

As I mentioned in the story Pearl's place is east of Bancroft. Stay on Highway 62 east to Maple Leaf. The House of Dolls is on the left. There's no official admission charge, but you can bet your bottom dollar you'll want to leave something in the box provided for voluntary contributions. You'll love it!

The Simple Life

🍒

There's much to be said for the simple life. A life uncontaminated by worldly goals and worldly ways or urban living.

Farmer Ken Genrick keeps it simple. Although farming can become a pretty complicated and discouraging proposition these days, Ken operates his farm in Renfrew County just about the way his great-grandfather did in the last century.

Ken and his wife, Doreen, are happy people. They live in the same log house built by Ken's ancestors in 1888. They raised their family there. The original barns still house their livestock. The only modern piece of equipment to be seen is a rather old tractor. They have always been debt-free. If they want to buy something, they save for it. It's a simple life and, as Jenny put it, "they know who they are."

A trip to the Genrick farm is a trip back in time. I leaned against an old split-rail fence and looked out on the surrounding countryside

—the nearby lake, the hills and forest primeval of the Ottawa Valley. Ken's great- grandfather, German immigrant Earnest Genrick, had slashed his way through dense bush country, cut the trees to build a cabin, and tilled the unyielding soil. His wife and young son helped him. Now Ken's children and, at times, his youthful grandchildren, help him run the farm.

Mind you, the Genricks have some modern conveniences. Ken's wife has an up-to-date kitchen, although she still uses the original fruit cellar and makes choke cherry and apple jelly. But Ken decided to stay with the old ways where actual farming is concerned.

There are four horses in one of the barns. They are often hitched to a plow if the tractor breaks down, and are always used for hauling logs. And Ken's blacksmith shop is available. He was shoeing one of the horses the day we were there. Down by the lake is an ancient sawmill and Ken says it still does its job efficiently.

There are 18 pigs, some beef and dairy cattle, chickens, a few fields of grain and a big vegetable garden. As a result, the family is largely self- sufficient for basic food needs.

Like everyone else, the Genricks have their ups and downs, but the simplicity of their lifestyle minimizes the difficulties.

I asked Ken if it was possible for a young farmer to start from scratch and survive in today's market.

"It's possible if he inherits a farm outright and remains debt-free," he said. "But he also has to love this life."

Getting There

From Bancroft take Highway 28 east for about 30 miles to Highway 514. Go straight ahead for about a mile. You'll see Genrick Road on the left. They're a great family.

When The Heat's On

After 30 years of service, John Hickey retired from the Etobicoke Fire Department and returned to live in his birthplace of Galway Township in the Haliburton Highlands. It so happened they were trying to start a volunteer fire brigade in Galway at the time and asked him if he'd become a chief.

Like an old firehorse answering the call, he said he'd do it. But only for six months. That was 15 years ago, and as he says, "It was a long six months." Then he retired for the second time. He was 81 years of age and thought to be Canada's oldest fire chief!

That was when I met Chief Hickey, and a lot of water has passed through the hoses since his firefighting career began. He'd been with the old Long Branch Brigade in the '30s before going to Etobicoke, and he'd seen plenty of action, with his most vivid recollections being those of Hurricane Hazel.

He showed me a picture of himself receiving a long service medal from John Aird, a former Lieutenant-Governor of Ontario, and an impressive gift his Etobicoke colleagues had given him when he retired. It was a sculptured old-time fire engine complete with horses and an engraved tribute to go with it.

John said that the Galway Volunteer Brigade had started with one truck and just a few trainees, but since then had grown to boast a staff of 26. The volunteers are scattered around the township and in the event of a fire, the Chief's main job is to direct operations from an intercom system set up at the station. That isn't to say John couldn't take an active part if he had to. Despite his advanced years, he appears to be about 60 at the most. He was lean and lithe and fit as a fiddle.

I asked him what he intended to do since he'd finally taken the plunge into the strange tribal custom we call "retirement."

"I'll likely be doing what I intended to do in the first place. Go fishing," he said. "After that, I want to keep some bees and also get back to my landscape painting. And I have three hens and a rooster that keep me hopping."

Maybe this time he'll make it, and won't be going from the frying pan into the fire. But even now he'll still be on call -- as a consultant. That is, when the heat's on.

Sugarbush Bunnies

❦

Out in the country amid the rolling hill of Mono Mills, east of Orangeville, live the "Sugarbush Bunnies." They're not the usual type of bunnies. They're fluffy angora rabbits all puffed up with angora wool, one of the softest animal fibres.

They're kept in a couple of outbuildings behind the Bolce family home. The buildings are near a sugarbush on the property. Hence the name for the rabbits.

Believe me, Barbara Bolce is kept busy taking care of the bunnies. Her children are now grown, her husband Paul is self-employed and work at home, so taking care of her charges has become almost a full-time job.

When I was there, she had over 50 English angoras, considered the darlings of the angora world, and three French angoras. On top of that, there were 15 little ones, three weeks old, and six others 10 days old. I held one in the palm of my hand. Its eyes were slightly open. It was just beginning to see the light of day.

The adult English angoras have heavy wool on their faces, ears and feet. They're cozy-looking little critters. The French angoras are one of the oldest breeds. They have lots of wool on their bodies, but have smooth faces and ears.

Some of the rabbits are kept outside in spacious cages, and there's a space where they can run around. They're fun to watch and very friendly. They make great pets and can be house broken.

They moult every three months. It's essential that they be sheared or plucked, otherwise they lick off their fibre which fills their stomachs. Then they can't eat and may even starve.

With a bunny sitting placidly on her lap, Barbara spins its wool right into the spinning wheel. Photo by Paul Bolce.

Barb plucks rather than shears the rabbits. Each plucking yields about three ounces of wool. She takes it inside and goes to work with her spinning wheel.

But very often she'll carry a rabbit into the house, and with it sitting placidly on her lap, spins its wool right into the spinning wheel. No middle man. She makes angora hats, mitts, scarves and stuffed animals.

Although she sells the items at fairs and shows, Barb figures she breaks about even considering the work and expense of caring for the angoras. She looks upon it as an absorbing hobby, not a bunny making proposition.

Getting There

Take Highway 400 north to Highway 9. Go west toward Orangeville. About 15 miles over you'll come to Highway 50. You're getting close. Keep going on Highway 9 to Adjula Road 2. You'll see the Granite Art Gallery on the right. The Bolce family lives in the big brick house right next door.

Ontario's Breadbasket

T en thousand years ago, give or take an eon or so, the last Ice Age played one of its final fancy tricks, and in a farewell gesture drained a big lake about 50 miles north of what's now Toronto.

A forest of trees, bullrushes and grass sprung up, and as it died, left layers and layers of muck soil beneath a shallow covering of water.

For years it was just another marsh. The thought of cultivating it appeared ridiculous. But in the early '30s, eighteen families from Holland arrived in the area. They were experienced farmers who knew more than the rest of us about dikes, irrigation and so forth.

They set to work and, using time-honored methods, created Holland Marsh, which has become known as Ontario's Breadbasket.

The mighty muck, chock full of organic matter, was black gold for the Dutch farmers. Black and beautiful. Eventually, 44% of Canada's onions came from the marsh, and 22% of our carrots. Thanks to that old black magic, it's now our biggest vegetable garden.

The thousands who travel up Highway 400 to cottage country are familiar with the marsh. The highway slopes down and cuts through the sprawling 16-mile spread where at harvest time celery, lettuce, carrots and onions grow row upon row as far as the eye can see.

But there's a lot more to the marsh than meets the eye. A few miles to the east is the little village of Ansnorvelt, where some of the early settlers still live. In the springtime, tulips bloom in the tidy gardens and many people wear wooden shoes.

There are 167 farms in all, with the average holding 40 acres. One of the larger farms is owned by John Verkaik. His grandfather was one of the original settlers and bought the property for $25 an acre. It's now worth about $10,000 an acre. John employs up to 25 people to harvest his carrots and celery, and is one of the few to package the produce right on the spot.

Close to the highway is an unobtrusive building that houses what's been an important aid to the marsh farmers for over 40 years. It's the Muck Research Station where scientists study insect control and crop diseases among other things.

The chief scientist is Mary Ruth McDonald. She's young, knowledgeable and knows the marsh and its people like the back of her hand. She's always on call and, if a farmer has crop problems, she hops in her pickup truck and is off and running to see how she can help. She was telling us that, if properly handled, the old marsh can be productive for another 200 years.

By the way, contrary to popular opinion, Holland Marsh wasn't named after the Dutch farmers, but for Major A. Holland, an army man who surveyed the area in 1830 at the request of Lord Simcoe.

Getting There

You're likely familiar with the Marsh if only at a distance. To get to the Muck Station turn off Highway 400 at Canal Road and double back on the service road. To reach Ansnorvelt stay on Canal Road and go east a few miles.

The Queen Bead

Beads have been around for over 30,000 years. They've been used for a variety of things, and once were a medium of exchange.

That's what Dorothy Hunter was telling me. And Dorothy should know. She's a bead expert, and has what must be the largest privately owned collection of beads anywhere.

The walls of the basement in her Peterborough home are lined with thousands of boxes crammed with beads. Each box is meticulously labelled with the type and size of beads it holds. There are smaller boxes secreted in the kitchen, more in the sunroom and even some under the beds. Altogether there are millions of beads.

Dorothy, now in her late '70s, puts the beads to good use. She makes necklaces, earrings and bracelets of great beauty and fine craftsmanship. She sells them at shows, but also has quite a clientele for custom work, and helps customers coordinate their wardrobes with beads.

The bead business began in a modest way. Some years ago she began to dabble in macrame and embroidery. For a bit of variety she did some bead work, as well as background study about the history and uses of beads.

One day while shopping, she heard about a jewellery firm that was going out of business. It was 1970 and beads weren't particularly popular, so she was able to buy the company's huge collection for a song. She had hit the jackpot! As she put it, "It was the bead buy of the century."

It took one truck, three carloads, and a full day of passing boxes through the basement window to install the haul in the Hunter home.

"After that I went commercial," she laughed, "And now it's almost a full-time job."

She has a long table where some of her work is displayed for visitors. There are necklaces and also off-beat things like a shark's tooth on a shell, and a butterfly made of shells she picked up on Atlantic shores.

She works with beads as large as 20 mm down to those scarcely 1 mm. It's often a time-consuming, detailed task. Using braided nylon lines, she stiffens the ends and pokes the lines through the beads. It looked to me as if it would require the patience of a saint.

Needless to say, Dorothy often wears beaded accessories. It's easy for her to be decked out like a queen, and with that massive collection and her skill in the craft, she is indeed the Queen Bead.

Getting There

Dorothy lives at 712 Armour Road in Peterborough. Phone 705-743-4091. Her displays of beads are outstanding.

Ken's Collection

❦

Every morning Col. Ken Willcocks strides over from his big home on the banks of the York River, which cuts through the village of Bancroft, to his motel which is about a hundred yards from the house.

He's lean, lithe and erect. A military bearing. That's natural enough. He was a career soldier in England, and has been aide de

Part of the big collection of swords is displayed in a showcase in the motel. Ken's first sword was given to him by his father. Photo by Rick Dade.

campe to six of Ontario's Lieutenant Governors. He's also a collector of swords. When he and his wife, Lenore, bought the motel, they called it "The Sword" and the collection was used as a motif.

When you register, you see a huge sword hanging on the wall behind the front desk. It always reminds me of the kind worn by the Knights of the Round Table.

But the bulk of the collection is hung in a showcase in the hall as you go towards the dining room. There are swords of all kinds. There must be 50 of them. Some date back a couple of centuries. A few of the swords were made in recent years. One is called "The Olympic Sword," and was given to Pauline McGibbon when she officiated at the opening of the Olympic sailing in Kingston some years ago. Another was presented to Ken when he retired as president of the

Ontario Motel Association. And there's one used in the Wilkinson Razor commercial that was seen on television.

Ken's first sword was given to him by his father the day he was commissioned in the British Army. The ceremony, by the way, was performed by Princess Elizabeth, now the Queen. Since then, he's been collecting all types of swords, cutlasses and bayonets.

The bayonets and daggers are fixed to a wall in the coffee shop. Visitors are intrigued by them. One dagger was designed by two commandos named Skyes and Fairbairn. It's made to fit between a commando's shoulder blades, and could be drawn if one of the daring raiders of the Second World War was in extreme difficulty.

On one of the panels are several miniature soldiers. They were made in England and are quite authentic. Some go back to the days of the Crusades, and others depict various types of warriors right up to World War II.

I always sit in the last booth in the coffee shop where I write scripts and stories. Since I'm sort of a fixture, there's a photo of me on the wall above the booth entitled ''Bill Bramah's Bancroft Office.''

Every once in a while I take a break and wander around looking at the swords. The story behind each one is fascinating -- an insight into the cutting edge of history.

Getting There

There are several ways to get to Bancroft. It's at the junction of Highway 62 north and 28. Highway 62 becomes the main street which is Hastings. The Sword Motel is a few blocks down on the left.

The Artisans

Nestled amid the beauty of the Kiwartha Lakes in the village of Lakefield, a few miles from Peterborough, the Otonabee River cuts through the centre of the busy little community which has a turn-of-the-century charm that visitors invariably find appealing.

There are some interesting shops on the main street, and many buildings from bygone days, like the tiny Christ Church built of stone in 1854 by volunteers of many faiths. The village is also home of Lakefield College School, famous for its royal students like Prince Andrew and Prince Philip of Spain.

Among the shops on the main street is one called "The Artisans." It's where 28 artists and craftspeople from the area display their work. It's a small shop. Some of the artisans work right there upon occasion, but mostly they just drop off what they want to display, and then go back to their individual studios. They take turns minding the store, share the rent, and share their artistic talents.

What sets them apart is the variety of things they do and the wide range of their ages. But most of all their unbridled exuberance!

I first heard about them when I had a letter from April Sherwood, one of the original organizers. It was written in longhand in a racy style as if the writer was breathlessly conveying the message. She ended the letter with "please excuse the writing, my enthusiasm outweighs my ability with a typewriter."

I chuckled as I read it, and later when we went over to meet the artisans she had described, I was immediately caught up in the buoyant spirit of it all.

About 10 of the group had crammed into the little shop for a TV story we'd planned. Each of them had picked out a cubbyhole where they'd set up their easels and other tools of their crafts.

They were a motley crew. Somehow, cameraman Kevin Smith, who was with us that day, managed to squeeze his equipment into the various nooks and crannies members of the crafty band had chosen.

Potter Margaret Fish, who was in her '80s, was working beside two young artists, Jim Rowe and Donald Craig. Donald paints scenic watercolors and Jim creates acrylics on canvas. Some of his works are often used for graphics in The Toronto Star.

We had a lot in common with Larry Glover, a retired TV producer, who now spends his time ''working over a hot iron,'' as he put it, making attractive stained glass creations. He gave Jenny a hummingbird he'd made, and it now graces one of our kitchen windows at the farm.

In another corner Patti Briggs was weaving magic on her loom. Nearby was Glen Nicholas, a former World War II commando who now lives a gentler life as a potter. And of course, April was there, organizing things with that boundless energy I'd sensed in her letter.

We spent the day at ''The Artisans'' shop. As Jenny said while we were driving off, ''They're inspiring. I think it's because of their sheer love of life.''

Getting There

Lakefield is just a few miles from Peterborough. The shop is about halfway down the main street. It's well worth a visit.

Spinning Wheels

Gerald LeBlanc has been a woodworker for 20 years. He learned the craft from the ground up, working with his father in the woodlots of Nova Scotia.

But a few years ago while he was making cabinets for a city sky-scraper, his mind went back to his childhood days in the Maritimes. He remembered his grandmother sitting at her spinning wheel making socks and mitts for loggers. He sensed a desire to return to a simpler life.

As he mulled over these recollections, it occurred to him that no one seemed to be making spinning wheels like his grandmother's anymore. You could find them in antique shops, but in many cases they were in disrepair and no longer useful.

As a hobby Gerald started to make Saxony spinning wheels similar to the ones his grandmother had. He sold a few of them, and then last year opened a business in his garage and began making them on a full-time basis. Appropriately, he called the business "My Acadian Heritage." He and his partner Marilyn Carlton, who handles the marketing, found there was a wide open field for the product.

In his workshop in Markham, Gerald makes every piece of the spinning wheels by hand. They're of solid maple and a fine-looking piece of furniture, but just as important, are excellent for spinning.

I stood beside him as he prepared the maple for the lathe. He moved to another machine to make the base of the distaff, as it's called.

Gerald kept up a running commentary about the procedure, and I nodded periodically to give the impression I understood what was going on. Meanwhile, Marilyn was over in a corner of the workshop, varnishing one of the finished products.

"Most new wheels these days don't stand up for long," she said, "But these will last for generations."

Gerald says he will never mass produce the spinning wheels, which the couple call "The Rumpelstiltskin" as a tradename.

The partners can tell some good yarns about the problems they faced when they started. But they unravelled them and opened up a new market by putting a new spin on an old craft.

Getting There

Gerald lives at 27 Wales Avenue in Markham. The phone number is 905-472-3952. It's just a short spin from the Markham Museum at the north end of the main street. Give him a call first.

Firefighter's Museum

It took me back to my childhood days. Suddenly, I became a curly-headed five-year-old who was being held up to stroke the manes of Pat and Mike. They were the two big horses who pulled the firetruck when the alarm went off at the fire hall on Lake Street in St. Catharines.

Bubs has been curator since the museum opened. Some of the old firefighting equipment goes back to the turn of the century. Photo by Rick Dade.

But I was in Port Hope at the Canadian Firefighter's Museum. And what sparked these heady recollection was all the firefighting gear of yesteryear. Bubs Town, our guide, must have noticed the faraway look in my eyes. "Takes you back, doesn't it?" she smiled.

Bubs (her real name is Adelaide but everybody calls her Bubs) has been curator of the museum since it was opened by the Ontario Fire Buffs Association some years ago. She's a knowledgeable lady who can reel off all sorts of facts and figures about the hundreds of antique items gathered from various parts of Ontario.

She showed us horse-drawn vehicles that went back as far as 1881, and a hand-drawn chemical unit from 1907. Then there were the trucks -- 15 of them. John Holden, one of the founding members who happened to be there at the time, said the members were especially proud of one from Peterborough. Built in 1927, it was the first motorized truck in the Kawarthas area.

The other paraphernalia was also intriguing. We saw the asbestos outfits worn by firemen 50 years ago. They were so heavy, a hoist was needed to get them on.

Over in a corner were a number of fire extinguishers of the sodium acid type used in the '30s and '40s, and glass globe extinguishers you'd hang on the wall of your home. They were made of pear-shaped colored glass and filled with carbon tetrachloride. It's now known they were dangerous and caused liver and kidney damage.

Fire buffs from various parts of the world have visited the museum. It's the second largest of its kind in the country. The larger one is in Nova Scotia.

Cameraman Rick Dade got Bubs to put on some old firefighting regalia and took shots of her at the wheel of a truck. Since she's a tiny woman, the coat was dragging on the ground as she clapped around in the big rubber boots.

I was curious about how she became involved in the project. "My grandfather was a fireman," she said, "And I live across from the fire hall and I've always been interested in the work and equipment. It's been a labor of love here and during the summer months I'm on the job seven days a week, but I wouldn't have it any other way.''

And what does her husband think of it all?

''He doesn't mind. He's a lawn bowler,'' she laughed.

Getting There

Take 401 to Highway 28 at Port Hope. Go south. You're on Ontario Street. About a mile down veer to the left to Mill Street. Follow Mill Street down to the waterfront. The Museum is on the left in some old buildings.